LOVE
UNLIMITED

Virgin

BARRY

LOVE
UNLIMITED

INSIGHTS ON LIFE
AND LOVE

WHITE

WITH MARC ELIOT

First published in Great Britain in 2000 by Virgin Books
an imprint of Virgin Publishing
Thames Wharf Studios
Rainville Road
London W6 9HA

First published in the USA by Broadway Books

A catalogue record for this book is available from the British
Library.

ISBN 1 85227 818 8

Printed by Butler & Tanner Ltd, Frome and London

FOR MY MOTHER

Contents

LOVE
UNLIMITED

ONE

LOOKING FORWARD AND LOOKING BACK

"I'VE GOT SO MUCH TO GIVE"

Now that I'm here, no more tears
Come here, come here
And you won't find
Things that broke your heart
And threw your mind,
Not here, no, not here . . .

To you, my dear,
I've got so much to give,
It's gonna take my lifetime,
Gonna take years and years and years and years—

I WRITE PASSIONATELY *about love. It is my grand theme, and music is my special lady. Listen as I do to the one you love, the one who loves you, and you will learn everything you need to know. Love will bring you many fortunes. It will bring you the emotional understanding you never had before, as it overlays meaning with feeling. It will make you flexible and will breed compassion. It will teach you and your baby to talk things over rather than fight them out. Understand, love will make you look at yourself in so many different ways . . . the way I am looking at you now.*

I'm here, my lady, you don't have to be sad anymore. Love will renew itself, if you give it the chance. I'm here to stay, I'm not going anywhere. I'm going to be with you for a lifetime. You are my passion. This is the message behind my music—it is about a love that endures, that is loyal and true, that is full of passion. An all-consuming love, it is about a pure world every person wishes he or she could live; the finest world I know.

I write sheet music, baby, for use in your temple of love. The patterns are simple and direct, like the purity and the glory of love itself.

Come here, baby . . . oh come here . . .

. . .

THIS BEAUTIFUL AFTERNOON I am sitting on my terrace overlooking the peaceful waters of the great Pacific Ocean. I am relaxing in the afternoon of my life, a life that has taken me from the hard, mean streets of South Cen-

tral Los Angeles to the fantastic, unbelievable heights
of love, romance, fame, and
fortune. The sun is just
beginning to think about
dropping into that gorgeous
Pacific blue, and I am kicking back, thinking of how
I got so far, to this place
of comfort and relaxation,
of beauty and satisfaction.
Surely it has been a long
road, but worth it. And I
look forward to all that still
lies ahead.

This fabulous journey
atop the first-class wings of fame began for me in 1948 when the music I
have always heard inside my head first found an outlet through the special
sound of my unique, God-given voice. Making music wasn't something I
"learned." Creating a sound of distinction isn't something anybody learns,
no matter how many music lessons your parents forced upon you when
you were a kid, no matter how many songs you listen to when you're in
bed with your lover.

Music is something that learns you!

Ever since I was a little boy, whenever I heard a song on the radio I
liked, I made it my song. If I was alone, I immediately formed an attach-
ment to it, a touchstone to the time and place I first heard it. If I was with
a lady, it became a clear reminder to me of whom I was with, how I felt
about her, and how she felt about me. Songs became the bridges between
my romantic stepping-stones. Later on, when I started recording, my own
music served as the bridge-builder for lovers everywhere. I had found my
sound of distinction, and it became the property of lovers all over the
world, linked by the universal appeal of my words of love set to the
rhythm I felt and took from life.

I've often been asked to analyze the appeal of my music, something I've always hesitated to do. A song is like a car engine; it runs only when all the elements are intact. Take it apart to study the nuts and bolts, and all you have are nuts and bolts. Perhaps, then, the best way to tell you about it is what my fans have always told me. I trust my audience. They know what they like, and it is from them I have always found the best "meanings" of my songs. Most often I've heard it said my music has a primal sexuality, which is identified and expressed through my voice and sense of rhythm. My music has a definite appeal that helps put people in the mood for romance. I believe that every black person has this rhythm, but very few know how to use it the way I could—first as a dancer and later on as a musician. Anyone who can use that rhythm, sing, dance, play congas, play an instrument, always has been highly respected by others, because not everyone can do it. A Barry White record is lipstick and perfume for the soul, a magnum of fine-vintage champagne to be poured directly from one heart into another.

Something that has always made my music so special is its strong appeal to both men *and* women. Black men, black women, white men, white women, Latinos, it appeals to one and all.

So many women from every walk of life have told me that my music exactly captures their personal philosophy toward men, how I represent to them the gentle, understanding, and caring lover they imagine in their hottest dreams; that it helped locate the gentle, warm, intimate side of themselves. In that sense, I'd have to say that my music has always been more a woman's *thang*. They like to say to their boyfriends that they can tell just from listening to me that "Barry knows how to make love to a woman!" So, yes, my music sends a strong and clear message of love that speaks directly and intimately to ladies. *Come on, darlin', Barry's here. . . . The time is right for us to be together. . . .* They'll tell me how through my voice I seem actually to be in the boudoir with them. Some have even said they have to turn on the light to make sure it's just a CD playing and that I'm not really there.

The men, meanwhile—let's just say they know me as their lady-catcher. Time and time again they tell me about how, when they were after a woman and couldn't get her, they'd slip a Barry White tape into the cassette player and it was all over. The ladies insist they hear something in my voice they are attracted to—the sound of it and the way I say things the men they're with don't quite know how to express. I wind up doing the talking and the seducing for the men. Whenever men meet me in person, they always tell me the same kind of thing. "I can't believe it's you, Barry. You are *the man!*"

The thing I love to hear most usually goes something like this: "You know, Barry, my wife and I made a baby to your music," or "I got married to your music." It doesn't get any better for me than that! I have come to be called the *Guru of Love!*

Of course I appreciate the title, but the truth is I'm not their guru, or anybody's for that matter. I'm simply a man who writes *with* love, *for* love and lovers of all faces, races, creeds, and beliefs. If I've produced some music that strikes a chord in the fine-tuned land of people's emotions, so be it. In that sense, my music is my great, special gift that allows me to create a more perfect world than real life. It takes us all out of the reality of the lives we live, into the fantasies of our dreams. It puts form and style to instincts and emotions. It gives the mystery of romance a rock-hard rhythm, a solid heartbeat, a signature of the soul.

I do it in part because of my essential romantic nature. Songwriting taps that deep well within me, and I use my voice as the instrument to send it out. The unique sound and resonance of my voice is the best special ingredient, that bottom "low-note" appeal. It's rough, but yet *not* rough. Tough but gentle. Macho yet sensual. Huge yet intimate. Manly, in a humble way. It is my supreme gift; the gilded chariot, if you will, upon which I have driven the music of my life.

Naturally, I didn't always have the voice I have now. Until I was fourteen years old I had a sound not unlike the famous high-pitched voice of Michael Jackson. When adolescence hit me, my sound didn't go down to a tenor, the way most boys' do, and stay there. Mine went down *twice,* first to a first tenor and then to a bass singer, that second one like a drop off the Empire State Building. The change came overnight. One morning I woke up with my new voice and hair all over my face. My mother called me over and examined my cheeks and chin closely, with her eyes and fingertips. "My God," she said. "My baby has become a man!"

Once my voice dropped, there was no escaping its power. Everywhere I went I could see the immediate effect it had on people. It always took me by surprise and would continue to do so for many years, especially after I left the neighborhood. I'd be in an elevator and someone would call out for the floor. I'd say, "Top, please," and everybody's head would turn around to see where that voice was coming from. Or I'd pick up the phone to make a long-distance call, ask the operator for assistance, and hear back, "My, but you have a beautiful voice!" This happened to me wherever I went. I was uneasy at first, but eventually grew used to it.

Today I know that a great voice lies not purely in its sound but serves as an inspiration too, and the route to that inspiration is often instinctive, unplanned, mapped out deep in the soul. It leads you on the pathway to a special kind of deliverance—from the microphone of the studio to the soul of the world.

TODAY, IN MILES, I live in San Diego, not all that far from Los Angeles, where I grew up. However, in time, this is a journey that has taken me a lifetime to make. Although I have always considered myself a native Angelino, I was, in fact, born in Galveston, Texas, where my mother happened to be visiting relatives.

My given name was Barry Eugene Carter. I actually had two legal names—that of my father, whose family name was White, and that of my mother, whose family name was Carter. It seems when my mother returned to Los Angeles, my daddy, who had a wife and family on the other side of town, saw her name, Carter, on my birth certificate and was not happy about it. When my parents first met she thought she had found the man of her dreams. She was sure they'd get married sooner or later, which, of course, because he already was, they never could. However, he did want me to carry his name. So he took my birth certificate, scratched out "Carter," and substituted "White." That's the name I was given, and that's the name I have to this day.

My father came around every now and then, although he was never there as much as any of us would have liked. He'd come in, throw some money down, and leave. You see, he had this other family, and there was just so much bread and dad to go around. I learned early on not to depend on my father for certain things,

because he was just not going to be there all the time for me. I can remember comforting my mother the nights she cried about how she hated that we didn't have a real father living with us at home.

Two people I did love very much, and who were far more visible, were my mother's two brothers, Uncle Eddie and Uncle Jimmy. They both came often to visit. Both were self-educated, and both shared their knowledge with us. One of the greatest things they taught us was how to be unselfish.

Uncle Eddie was from San Francisco, while Uncle Jimmy lived all the way in Chicago. Uncle Jimmy had a family and worked as a Pullman porter for the railroad, a job that brought him to Los Angeles once a month. We were so poor that the only time we were sure we were going to eat was when Uncle Jimmy came. We'd clean the house from floor to ceiling, to make it nice for him, and he'd share his money and his time with us.

So you see, Barry White came into this world riding in the coach

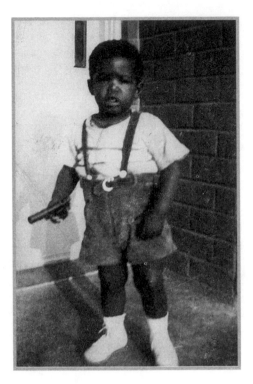

section of the soul train. How I got my ticket punched into the first-class supersonic section, well, that wondrous journey is the story of my life.

Let me begin it by telling you about a very strange and wonderful phenomenon I've experienced. Up front, I should make it clear that I am not a conventionally religious man. For that matter, I believe in very few conventions—of the heart, mind, or soul. Rather, I have been guided by a *Voice* that has been inside my head all my life. This *Voice,* which, as you will see, takes many forms, and has guided me with a spirit and sureness I've tried my best to obey.

Sometimes the *Voice* comes through other bodies, other souls, but always I know it when I hear it, and I listen when it talks to me. Hear me now as I hit the replay button and slip back to the opening track on the album of my life—the first time I hear the word and the *Voice* of my supreme and beautiful guide.

It was April 1959, I was fifteen years old and a very bad boy. The police, having grown tired of dealing with my street crap, finally decided to throw me in jail. Because I wouldn't turn sixteen until September, I was still, if barely, a juvenile in the eyes of the law, a circumstance for which, as it turned out, I would soon be very grateful.

My mama, Sadie, my younger brother, Darryl, and I were all living in a small house in West Los Angeles, over on 42nd Place and Hoover. Darryl's full name, by the way, was Darryl Lionel White, after Darryl Zanuck, a name Mama fell in love with when she was working at MGM. (Although I asked her many times, I have no idea where she got Eugene from. I wish I knew.)

Anyway, one Friday night some friends of mine came by and one of them suggested we grab some tires from Fletcher Jones' Chevrolet dealership and service headquarters. I'd never had crime partners before. For the past several months I'd been messed up over an emotionally crushing falling-out with my girlfriend, Mary, and because of it, had been going out on my own, burglarizing houses, fighting, drinking, and stealing cars.

Mary was a beautiful little neighborhood girl. We'd first met when I was in the eighth grade and she was in the seventh. We became childhood sweethearts, and anyone who knew Mary and me from the 'hood knew us as a couple in love. We were crazy about each other in that special private universe way only kids can be.

The first three years I'd gone with Mary, I'd never even *touched* her. When we finally consummated our love, we practiced the rhythm method, and for one of the very few times in my life I lost the beat, because one day I discovered that Mary was pregnant. We decided to have the baby, and I felt blessed when Mary gave birth to our first child, Barry, Jr. I still lived at home but spent a lot of time with Mary and Barry, Jr. Then Mary became pregnant again, and one summer afternoon I decided to pay her a visit. I walked over to her house and saw her sitting right there on her front porch *talking to another brother!* That's what messed me up! I felt betrayed, as if Mary had cheated on me behind my back. I was so hung up in my own definition of purity that I didn't want to ever see Mary even talk to another boy. To me, she was one of the most beautiful women I'd ever seen, with a soulful, slightly square elegance I'd found in no one else but my mother.

The fellow she was talking to that day happened to be a friend of mine. His name was Clifton, and all they did was talk. However, it was enough for me to take her off the pedestal I'd put her on. That's how pure her image was to me. I guess because I'd had my mother all to myself, in a way that Darryl never could, being in jail all the time, I wanted Mary the same way.

Make no mistake, I didn't blame Clifton for anything. He was, in fact, one of the brothers in on the tire job. No, I blamed Mary, wrongly of course, for what I took as this major betrayal. Even so, I knew I would never fall in love again with any other woman in that same, pure way. I would love again, of course, but not *fall in love.* When I told my mama about it she knew I'd made the same kind of mistake with Mary she had with my father, and that in both instances, it had nothing at all to do with the other person. It was the desire for a certain kind of perfection that is nearly impossible to achieve loving somebody. *And it was the wish to reach that type of perfection that became the basis for nearly every love song I would ever write.* That is why my next girlfriend became the only one I was ever able to find that perfection in. Her name? Lady Music.

As far as my feelings toward Mary were concerned, I didn't realize I was the one who'd changed. In truth, she was the same Mary she'd always been. That confusion messed me up so bad that for the next six months I became an alcoholic. I started drinking, acting mean toward people, stealing, doing things I'd never done before, even giving my mother bad mouth.

My bad behavior became something of an addiction. I'd sneak out of the house, steal a car, drive it around awhile, and then return it. This time the boys said we could make a lot of bread with these tires, so reluctantly I agreed to go along. Friday we stole them, Saturday we thought about all the money we were going to make off of them, and Sunday the police came to the house and took me away.

My poor mother didn't know what was happening, and it broke her heart because my younger brother, Darryl, only fourteen, was also in jail for something stupid *he'd* done. Darryl was already a veteran of the system, having gone to jail for the first time when he was only eight years old. My mother once told me she couldn't remember a single Christmas when Darryl was not locked up. It killed me to know her only two sons were inside and she didn't understand why, because she surely hadn't raised us to be that way. I felt so bad I didn't let her come and visit me the whole time I was locked up.

I really wasn't a bad kid at heart, I just didn't know any better. As a young boy with no father to act as a role model and set me straight, I couldn't help but get sucked into the street life. Between the two of us, it was my brother Darryl who was the truly unredeemable one, although we were both brought up in the mean streets, where the edge of danger and defiance carried an adolescent lure like an advertisement for macho. It made both of us want to be a part of something big and tough. It gave us false courage. It allowed us to think we could get away with anything until it was proven to us once and for all we couldn't.

It was a lesson I had to learn, and did, even as it robbed Darryl of a side of himself that could have made him a very successful person. You see, Darryl, like me, loved music. Every day he'd come home and ask if I'd heard this new song or that one. I firmly believe that if he hadn't fallen in love with crime as deeply as I fell out of love with it, he would have gone on to become a great musician in his own right. Hey, could we harmonize? Like you wouldn't believe! The White Brothers . . . what could have been . . .

Unfortunately, we didn't and it couldn't. Darryl had the ability but not the desire, and you have to have both to succeed in anything as difficult and demanding as show business. Instead, he walked with the attitude of a street cat, believing someone was always trying to do something to him or take something of his away. His nature was to be suspicious. There was no place in him for fear, and that is *not* a good thing, because a little fear can keep you a lot healthier. I guess the biggest difference between Darryl and me was our measure of, and stomach for, that fear.

Still, in order to defend myself from the hard threat of the streets, by the age of ten I started gang-banging. I learned how to fight, to defend myself from the bigger and tougher kids in the neighborhood. I became involved with the Businessmen (as in "taking care of business"), our local neighborhood street gang. The Businessmen were the oldest, baddest, and most envied gang in South Central, the one that every black boy wanted to be a member of. Our leaders knew all the coldest street ways. They were men who'd never grown out of low-riding and gang-banging. Everything we learned came from them, some of whom were *fifty-five years old.* Like I say, these dudes didn't kid around. No matter what was happening, they did it for keeps. Play boxing with each other could mean anything from a broken nose to an eye put out. When we fought for real outside the gang, these same warriors were willing to protect us with their own lives. They were, in a very real sense, all our missing fathers, as the streets became the only living rooms we ever felt comfortable calling home.

We had different approaches when we dealt with other gangs. We could reason with them, or we could fight. Most of the time we fought, or we'd be marked as easy victims. And I could fight, believe me. I learned early on the difference between whupping someone's ass, fucking him up, or killing him. I knew how to handle myself, but I only did it as a defensive thing, as a necessity for survival. Darryl, on the other hand, did it because he *loved* it.

My brother used to tell me that a lot of the Businessmen were scared of me because I was so quiet. It was true, I never said much, but when it came time, I let my fists do my talking for me. This gave me a mystique that inspired fear in some of the others, because they never knew what I was thinking. On top of that, at the age of fourteen in one extended spurt I grew to an imposing height of six feet three and a half inches, which helped to cut down the number of guys who wanted to tangle with me.

Still, I was always trying to understand the philosophy of the streets, to see if it differed in real life from what my mother had always tried to teach both Darryl and me, that fighting was *not* the way to go. I'll tell you something. Her words *stood up,* at least to me. Once I realized she was right, I concentrated on controlling my temper. I had a mean one, and knew if I didn't get a handle on it, I was going to be just like my brother.

Darryl, on the other hand, couldn't help himself. He loved to burn, to muscle up with rage. He craved the action of violence and could never get enough. Often, after we'd come home from hanging with the Businessmen in South Park, that's when me and him would get into it. I'd say something like "Man, that was fucked up what you did over there today," and he'd start swinging at me. We were almost the same size, maybe he was a little smaller than me, but that didn't matter. *Attitude,* that was what pulled him through. The attitude the street bred into you, tested every day of your life, gave you the weapon no one could take away. If you acted like you felt, that's how you became. If you acted scared you became scared. If you acted tough you were tough. And if you acted like you had all the confidence in the world, you'd find enough to stand up for any man or woman who needed you beside them when the going got rough. Attitude was the degree you picked up from the school of hard living, and Darryl and I both graduated with honors. And as with any degree, what you did with it was as important as getting it. Attitude could be a lifesaver or could get you killed. It was all in the knowledge of knowing how to use it. Those who knew survived, those who didn't lost everything, including, most times, their life. Attitude was something you wore constantly. Even then I knew guys half my size I wouldn't go near and some twice my size who wouldn't step foot on the same side of the street as me. *Attitude.*

I remember guys started picking on us when we were still little boys, six, seven years old. Darryl and I would go to the show, and they'd be waiting outside to take our money. I'd always just hand it to them, not willing (or able) to fight over something like that. My brother, though, remembered each and every one of their faces, and when he was all of thirteen, he hunted them down and brought them over to the house, one by one. I'd come home and my brother would be there with one of those guys.

He'd say, "Burly, remember this one?" Burly was my nickname for him, and also his for me, from when he was little and tried to call me "Buddy" and it came out Burly. It was our thing between us, the nickname we both used for each other.

"Yeah, Burly," I'd answer him. And then I'd say to the guy, "What's been happenin', man?"

"Oh, nothin'."

Then my brother would snap. *"You motherfucker,"* he'd say to him. "You used to take my—*BANG* . . ." and he'd hit him hard upside the head. One by one, he'd whup their asses.

By the time I was fourteen I couldn't go anywhere with my brother anymore, because everywhere we went he'd start trouble. He was bad, he really was. He and his partners liked to go out on the street and see who could punch the biggest *man* out cold. By the time he was in the penitentiary in Soledad he was knockin' out *bulls*. Who could hit the hardest, that was his thing. He lived a cold, brutal life. Only those who have a taste for blood can survive for very long that way. Seeing it so close to me, what it did to him, was one of the strongest reasons I had to want to resist a life of senseless street violence.

Ultimately, what saved me was the unconditional love I had for my mother. She was the kindest, most loving, most generous, and dearest woman in the world. The roots of the difference between Darryl and me lay in our parents. Darryl had the tough cynicism of the old man, while I had my mother's tender spirit and soul. When I was still a little boy, my father once told Darryl and me, "Don't ever do anything and not get paid for it." He was adamant about this. My mother, who was sitting right behind him, came around and said, "No, don't tell them that." Then she turned to Darryl and me and said, "Don't always do things and expect you have to get paid for it."

To this day, I see people making choices in life about their work, their art, their homes, their families. They either go my father's way, or they go my mother's. And the results they achieve usually can be followed with a fair amount of predictability. Character, indeed, becomes their fate, character that is determined at such an early and influential time in our lives.

Even though she didn't have very much, she always made us feel close and important. My mother was *everything* to me. She taught me, through her generous love and understanding, what it meant to take care of others, to not fear feeling gentle, to take pride in being the provider and the protector, and not to be afraid to identify with the feminine side we all have in us. My mother was my saving grace, my redeemer, the one who taught me that the nature of true love was unqualified, all-encompassing, and filled with endless amounts of what I think of still as spiritual passion.

Every Easter, no matter how poor we were—and we were so poor that one time I had nothing to eat but eggs for nearly a month and a half, breakfast, lunch, and dinner—Mama somehow found enough money to buy Darryl and me new blue suede shoes. I *loved* those shoes. I always wore them to Easter services at church, and one year I noticed this little girl named Josephine and her sister talking to Mama. Everyone could plainly see that they didn't have on very nice clothes. My mother found a way to take care of them all with new holiday outfits as well. I loved that about her.

Every night she used to come to our room and read to Darryl and me from the Bible. I learned all the stories but had a hard time believing them. So much of what I heard, even at that very young age, sounded to me like man-made morality tales meant to give hope to the hopeless, which so many at our church really were. I could never understand how one minute they could be praying, the next stealing money or pulling guns and razors out on each other. Who were all these people, I wondered, calling up and singing to God and Jesus every Sunday and for the six other days bloodying up the streets? Every day I saw things happen that banged up my young soul—violence, killings, the senseless maiming of people, the cruelty that men from the 'hood always showed to their women.

I began to understand that my faith was going to have to come from within, and if it was strong enough, nothing and nobody around me could ever shake it. Either I came to believe in myself or I didn't, and all the rest of it was . . . *stories. Stories told from man's, not God's, point of view.*

Gradually I started questioning everything I was taught about the Bible, in my early journey to discover who I really was and who I really

wasn't. Even before my voice changed, my mind did. I started reexamining in depth the Old and New Testaments. I also discovered the Holy Koran and the Holy Kabbalah, great works that made me question apparently contradictory parts of the Bible. Why, for instance, did the Old
Testament preach "an eye for an eye, and a tooth for a tooth" and the New
one that we should "turn the other cheek"? What changed God's mind?
Nothing! God didn't write the Bible, man did. It was man who changed *his*
mind.

As a young boy I saw these contradictions played out in front of my
eyes every Sunday. One time I noticed a big Cadillac illegally double-
parked. The fancy-clothed owner came out of the dry-cleaning store, and
a black woman walked up to him carrying some Jehovah's Witness *Watchtower* copies and tried to get him to buy one. The only problem was, he
was a pimp. "Why you out here selling *Watchtower?*" I heard him say. "You
ought to be selling pussy for me and fuck all this Jehovah's Witness shit!"

I was so offended by that! I slowed down, waiting to see what God
was going to do to this man for so badly disrespecting this lady.

Nothing. He did nothing!

The pimp drove off without incident. All day and into the night I
tried to understand why God did not come to this lady's rescue, and
couldn't come up with any answers that made sense.

One day Darryl and I came out of school and started walking down
Central Avenue. We passed this corner bar just as a dude came shooting
out the door onto the sidewalk, holding his neck. Blood was squirting out
of it. This tiny lady came out after him with the razor still dripping blood
in her hand. We both watched in silence as he tried to keep his head on his
body. He was walking all crazy, then he wobbled, then he fell over, dead
on the ground. *Where was Jesus now?* I wondered.

Then there were the Bakers, our next-door neighbors. Mr. and Mrs.
Baker were the sweetest couple, Monday till Friday. Every Friday evening
like clockwork they started fighting until by Saturday they were all cut
and bloody. I couldn't believe it. When Sunday night came they were always patching up each other's wounds, walking around with bandages all
over. "Mama," I asked one day, "what's wrong with those people?"

"Some are just like that," she said to me. *How can that be,* I wondered, *when Jesus is supposed to be in all of us?*

In spite of all my endless questions and growing doubts, Mama said going to church was the right thing to do, so I continued to go to services every Sunday, if for no other reason than to make her happy.

Besides, there was one part of it I really enjoyed. That was the music. I liked it so much one day I asked Mama if I could sing in the choir.

"Sure you can, baby," she said.

She arranged for me to join the junior choir, which rehearsed every Saturday. At first the others made fun of me, but what those kids didn't know was not only that I could sing, but *in harmony.* I had first learned how when I was only four years old, with Mama and Darryl, singing "Silent Night" in the perfect three-part harmony she taught us as we sat up in our pajamas in bed.

Once the seniors heard me sing, they wanted me in *their* group as well. I moved to the senior choir and just about blew the roof off the church. I guess you could say that's where I got my first taste of what it would be like to be a star. I noticed a murmur ripple through the congregation whenever it was my turn to sing. Soon enough, all they had to do was see me start to walk toward the mike and they'd start screaming and hollering.

One year I was invited by the church to recite "The Night Before Christmas." Afterward, Mama said one of the things that impressed her most that night was how I knew every word and didn't stumble a single time. "Your memory is tremendous," she said, and then made this prediction. "Barry, when you grow up, you are going to be one of the most dynamic speakers the world has ever heard. That's why I want you to always remember that whatever a man thinketh, so *is* he."

It didn't take long before I was the director of the choir. However, even as I continued to keep up with my choir duties, my private spiritual investigation deepened. Along the way I observed the behavior of others and plainly saw that in everyday life, people could and would disappoint you, and you would disappoint others and ultimately yourself. The difference being, if someone disappointed you, you felt like a fool. When you did it to others, you were a rogue. When you did it to yourself, you called it learning.

Right after my voice changed, some strange and fascinating things began to happen. As far as I was concerned, although I started going with Mary, there was still only one woman in the world good enough for me, and that was my mama. Darryl, on the other hand, had a million different ladies. His only problem was, he couldn't talk to them the way I could. I just had a natural ability to make a woman feel that she was on a pedestal. They'd call the house for Darryl, he'd pick up the phone and start talking, and I could hear him say everything wrong. He was either too aggressive, or he'd be cutting them off before they could say what they wanted to. Out of frustration one day he covered the receiver and said to me, softly, "Burly, talk to this bitch for me . . . in that way you have . . ."

From that moment on, whenever I'd walk in and Darryl was on the phone, he'd hand it to me and have me make believe I was him. I always knew immediately what to say. I'd grab the phone fast, before the girl could tell there was a change. After talking to them, they'd always say the same thing. "That's such a beautiful side of you, Darryl. I never heard you say anything like that before."

Darryl was always after me to teach him the "secret" of my way with women. I tried, without much success, to give him what my mother had taught me *very* successfully, that, in life, approach, like attitude, was everything. On the street, you needed attitude to survive. With a woman, you needed attitude to succeed. Same game, different playing board.

In a way, Darryl became the first in a series of "students" of love in need of a good talking-to that I counseled, while still a teenager myself.

One day a friend of mine who was much older than I was—he must have been maybe twenty-three or twenty-four—brought his girlfriend over to my house so I could speak to the both of them. I'd been giving him some street advice whenever I'd run into him because he liked to talk to me, one guy to another, about his problems. He'd take what I'd say, apply it to his relationship with his girlfriend, and the next time I'd run into him he'd tell me how much better they were getting along. "Man, it's amazing, everything you say is right."

All I was really doing was talking common sense. I told him what I thought he should do about his situation. How he should listen to what his woman was saying. How he should examine all the circumstances and see if there were answers he was missing. How he should look to himself for resolutions before looking to others for blame. He always began the same way, telling me he couldn't understand why he wasn't getting along with his girl.

"The first place you have to look for your mistakes," I told him, "is within yourself, not in her. She's reacting to whatever you're doing." Even at that early age, I believed something I still do to this day, and I guess it began with the way I felt my father treated my mother—that men don't understand women. We're always the aggressors. We're born with a fierce anger and a brute strength that we have to learn to control.

After a while, he asked if he could bring his girlfriend over to hear me say these things. There was something in the telling, he insisted, that made a difference. I agreed, and sure enough, a week later, they both came knocking at the door.

I invited them in, sat them down, and said, "What seems to be the problem?" He told me his side, she told me hers, and then I told them both what I thought they should do about it. Word started to spread, and by the end of the year I was counseling several neighborhood couples. And every time one of them came over they'd leave a few dollars, their way of saying thank you. I never asked for any money, they just gave it to me.

One day Mama came home early and wanted to know what was going on. She said she'd been hearing about these people being in the house while she was at work! I told her, "I'm counseling, Mama. Instead of going to work tomorrow, why don't you stay home? One of my couples is coming over. You can sit in the living room, listen, and watch."

Mama was skeptical at first. I was, after all, only fourteen. Besides, she was, understandably, leery of any outside grown-ups coming into the house, and rightfully so. Strangers were either salesman trying to sell you something you didn't need or the police looking for Darryl.

However, once she saw me do my thing, she became a believer.

By the end of that first year I was seeing twenty-two couples. I'd give them simple, commonsense advice. For instance, to couples who were fighting because the man was always leaving the house and not saying where he was going or when he was coming back, I'd tell them, "It's smart for people to know where you are, in case something happens to you."

I talked about things in a commonsense way, in such a fashion that both women and men could hear themselves through me. Years later, on *The Icon Is Love,* which I wrote and recorded in 1994, I have a song I partly based on my early experiences counseling these couples. It's called "Practice What You Preach":

> *You keep tellin' me this*
> *And tellin' me that.*
> *You say once I'm with you*
> *I'll never go back.*
> *You say there's a lesson*
> *That you wanna teach,*
> *Well, here I am baby,*
> *Practice what you preach!*

Another and completely different avenue in my personal spiritual quest began when I was fifteen years old. I was in the 'hood, about to cross the street, waiting (in every implied sense) for the light to turn green. My arms were filled with groceries I was bringing home for Mama. When the WALK sign flashed I stepped into the intersection. I didn't see anybody coming from the other side. I got halfway across when suddenly this elderly lady in a faded brown and shabby coat appeared *out of nowhere,* walking toward me. She didn't seem like she was doing very well. When we passed each other, she stopped, looked into my eyes, and smiled. I stopped as well and looked into hers.

"You're a Virgo child," she said to me out of nowhere in a soft, reassuring voice. I didn't know what she was talking about. I was Sadie's boy, and I was certain of it. Still, because my mother had always taught us to be respectful to our elders, I just shook my head and said "um-hmm."

"When is your birthday?" she asked, as we stood in the middle of the crosswalk.

"September twelfth."

"Yes, as I said, a Virgo child. You're going to be a great, great man one day."

"Excuse me, ma'am, but what's a Virgo child?"

"It means you're destined for greatness."

She continued crossing to her other side, and so did I. When I got to the corner, I turned to look one more time and she was gone. And I never saw her again.

I had to know what she meant. I started asking everyone what a Virgo child was, but no one knew. At first I thought it might have to do only with my birthday, until I learned it covered a couple of weeks before and after. This sparked an even greater level of curiosity in me. Eventually I began to put together the signs of the Zodiac with their meanings. I found out there were twelve different ones and was amazed how much people behaved like their signs described. I never became a fanatic about it, but from then on I started reading everything I could get my hands on.

Someone gave me a book by Linda Goodman, *Love Signs,* that I carried around with me for years. I practically *memorized* it. I couldn't believe how much was in there about me. Now, here was a book that I could *relate* to, that talked to me *about* me, not ancient men and women whom I was somehow supposed to relate to via the ancestral essence of my soul. *No, sir.*

It got to a point where I could talk to someone for a little while and make a pretty good call as to what their sign was. More often than not, I was right on the money.

NEVERTHELESS, IN SPITE OF the stars, the counseling, and all my efforts to separate myself from the violence and brutality of the streets, by the time I was fifteen and got arrested for stealing those tires, I'd been exposed to so much street negativity I was still in danger of becoming de-sensitized, of losing my way. The night they took me to Juvey (Juvenile) Hall I heard those gates close behind me, and it was the loudest *clang* I'd ever heard in my life. I'd never been locked up like this. I'd been busted for little things before, but my mother would always come and somehow get me out. Well, I knew my mother wasn't coming this time.

I *hated* being in jail. I didn't like people telling me what to do, when to get up, when to go to bed, what to eat, what not to eat, when to use the toilet, when *not* to use the toilet. And I hated not being home for my mama, who'd depended on me for so much. She didn't deserve having two sons behind bars.

After two months on the inside, it finally started kicking in. *I have to change my ways, because if I don't, I'm going to end up in jail the rest of my life!* All my partners and friends in the Businessmen were making a career out of going to jail. And here I was, just another bro from the 'hood locked up, shut down, not able to do anything I wanted to. Every night I kept thinking about something Darryl had once told me: When you start going inside, it's hard to break the habit. *Your partners are all there.* It's like being outside, only in. *Outside, only in.* That scared me.

It was a Wednesday night in May 1960 that changed my life. I went to bed, sank into my bunk, when all of a sudden out of the bleak stone-block nowhere down the hall from some other inmate's radio I started to hear this song. I'd heard it before, I don't know, twenty-five, thirty times, but it never hit me like it did that night. It was, of all people, Elvis Presley! The song? *"It's Now or Never."*

It became my personal message, meant only for me. *"Stop wasting your time, Barry,"* it said. *"When you get out you better change your ways. It's Now or Never!"*

I sat up in my cell bed and right then and there took an oath that I would do just that—change my life.

The next morning when I woke up everything around me looked and felt just a little bit different. I held onto that feeling until three months later, in August, when my court hearing finally came up. I was still determined to turn things around. Step number one was to get out of there. My immediate goal was to make sure I didn't go from Juvenile Hall to Soledad.

I was in the little holding room outside two courtrooms with all the other juvenile "bad" boys. Some went into this one where a certain judge was, and some went the other way. Everybody who went to the left was sent up. They'd come out and say, "Oh, man, I got twenty-two months . . ." Everybody who went to the right got a free pass home. Then *my* name was called—*Barry White*—and the man sent me to the *left!* My stomach flip-flopped, turned upside down and sideways. I was in such agony because I was sure I was going back inside!

I stood before Judge Hamilton (I know he won't believe I still remember his name, but that man made an *impression* on me!), the same judge who sent Darryl up. I knew who he was and, worse, *he knew who I was.* He was angry because my school record was so good, and he let me know it. He looked me straight in the eye and said, "You're not doing anything but conning your mother and now you're trying to con me, because we both know you know how to do the right thing."

I was scared as hell. The judge continued to give me a good old-fashioned tongue-lashing in his court, which to this day I can still hear in my head, especially when he looked at me and pulled the big switch. "I'm gonna let you go home, boy."

What?! My stomach did a *WHOOMMP!* I couldn't believe what I was hearing.

He went on. "Just remember, son, I'm gonna be your judge from now on, whenever you get in trouble. If you come back before me for so much as a jaywalking ticket you'll have twenty-two months to think about it." He stared at me coldly, pounded his gavel, and said, loud and with authority, "Probation for a year! Next case!"

I walked out of that courtroom with a big smile on my face. I passed through that same gate I'd heard slamming on me when I was going in, only this time it was slamming behind me. That same noise, *WHHHHRRAAAAAAHHHH,* but I liked it so much better from the outside. I knew I was never going back in, that the life I'd known on the street, all of it was history. I was going to change *everything,* because the night before I'd heard the *Voice and the Voice had heard me!*

The first thing I did when I got outside was to hug my mother. She was so happy she was crying, and you know what, I was crying too. I'd never been away from her like that for so long before. I knew what it had done to her and to me. Never again, I told myself. *Never again.*

She took me to the newest place I was to call home. While I was away Mama had moved to 48th and Avalon in South Central L.A., partly because of the rent and partly to try and keep me away from the Businessmen. As far as I was concerned, however, it was more than just a new address, it was a new day and a new ballgame. It was, in fact, a whole new song.

Two

A Place Called Freedom

Keep on, keep on doin' it
Right on, right on doin' it

I'll have to keep you pleased
In ev'ry way I can,
Gonna give you all of me,
As much as you can stand.
Make love to you right now,
That's all I want to do.
I know you need it, girl,
And you know I need it, too . . .

'Cause I'm never gonna give you up

I'VE GOTTEN CAR, *hotel, and front door keys sent to me in the mail from women with very explicit invitations. One even went so far as to contact me by phone willingly offering me her four or five daughters—at the same time. She wanted me to teach them, and their offspring, how to relate to men. I told her to tell her daughters what I tell everybody. Listen to yourself, your own heart, find your own voice of supreme guidance and you will learn all you will ever need to know. Hear it, trust it, follow it. I alone don't know anything you don't already know yourself. Don't be anything but proud, of yourself and your deeds, and loyal to the one you love, and you will find the reflection of that pride, love, and loyalty in your own heart.*

Loyalty! Once somebody loves you and allows you to move as freely as you want to, that's when all the temptations of living without limits begin. Freedom means the choice to live better, not worse. Freedom means the ability to choose love, not lust. You have to know when beautiful sex is a pathway to deep love, not the tawdry, cheapest, and greatest threat to it. Men and women will succumb to temptation and turn the intensity of feelings that have been awakened by love into a different kind of energy, something to catch new sexual partners. By doing so, they cheapen themselves, their very notion of what love is, and any respect they might once have had for the single, special person they think they are still in love with.

It is a high mountain to climb, the summit of love. It only takes one misstep to send you tumbling back in a flash, to the bottom, on your bottom, look-

ing up at where you once stood so regal and perhaps a little haughty. Remember, there are no free rides, no free passes in love. Even if no one else knows what you've been up to, you will. And believe me, no matter how clever you think you may be, if you know it, the one you love probably does as well. If you cheat on your lover, you are cheating on yourself. If you try to sneak out the back door of love, you will be shown the front door. Don't throw away what you have on something or someone you will never love. What's the point? You have to believe in the sanctity of love, and trust it. Remember—with love, if you abuse it, you will surely lose it.

·   ·   ·

I REALIZED EARLY on that changing my life was not going to be all that easy. Three days after I was released, a couple of my old friends from the 'hood came by. They weren't the Businessmen, like Mama feared, but three guys I used to sing with at lunchtime in school and harmonized with Friday nights on the corner. I let them in and one of them said, "Hey, Barry, man, you want to sing bass for us in the Upfronts? This guy in our group, he ain't makin' rehearsals. You can take his place."

The Voice!

I said, "Hell, yeah, man."

"We got this dude, Mr. Lummie Fowler, who's kind of like our manager and producer, writin' songs for us and everything . . ."

"Just show me where I'm supposed to go and tell me what you want."

Now, I'd always loved music but never thought about it seriously as something to *do.* I listened to the radio, had my collection of 45s, sang in church choir and on the corner, but never had any serious dealings with music until that day in 1960, when the Upfronts came knocking at my door and truly changed the direction of my life.

The next day I went over to Lummie's house to meet him. After the boys introduced me as their new bass singer we started right in rehearsing songs. A few days later Lummie said we were good enough and took us into the studio.

I'd never been in one before and was fascinated by the machinery of its heart and soul—the mixing board, which looked to me like nothing so much as a giant kind of robot lurking right there in the middle of the room.

"What is that?" I asked one of my friends.

"That's the board."

"What do you mean?"

"That's what records our music."

"Well, then, who is he?" I asked, pointing to the man behind it.

"The engineer. He runs the board."

"And those guys? The ones with the instruments in their hands?"

"Those are the musicians."

Real musicians!

I looked at their stuff. This was the first time I'd ever seen a drum kit close-up. *I liked it!* There was also a stand-up bass, a guitar, and a piano. I knew what a piano was because, although I'd never wanted to be a musician on it, I'd been playing Mama's since I was five years old.

At one time, she'd actually tried to give me lessons herself, but I hated it. I went crazy for two weeks trying to memorize scales. "That's all right," she said, when I told her I didn't want to do it that way. "You play any way you want." I discovered I could make that piano sing by figuring out with my fingers which chords pleased my ears. Music was something I had to feel rather than be taught. I'd sit in front of the radio, hear a song, and, after a couple of tries, figure it out. By the time I was eight years old, I could sing and play any song on the piano. It just came to me.

Even so, I never did it for the sheer pleasure. It was simply an instrument I found I could use to put what was in my heart out there by way of those black and white keys. One time when I was about twelve, I went to a party, and someone asked me to play the piano. I sat down and did a couple of songs, simple pop tunes like "In the Still of the Night." That's when I first learned you could become a hero in the ghetto another way, not by fighting, you see, but making music.

•   •   •

TO SEE ALL THESE instruments and equipment together was amazing. The instruments were like people, they had living souls to me. This was the exact opposite kind of place where I'd been confined for months, a jail filled with people who were soulless. Now I felt a pull inside of me, somehow hot and cool at the same time. I'd never felt anything like this before. I knew I'd walked into something, this little room cluttered with men, instruments, and machinery. They called it a studio. I called it freedom.

We got down to it and before long the Upfronts recorded its first song, an R and B thing we called "Little Girl." It didn't become a hit on the charts, but to me it was a smash! The *power* I felt from it! The *accomplishment!* On my personal chart it shot to number one *without* a bullet! I played it for my mother on my little phonograph, and when she was able to pick me out of the background singing bass, she said, "You did a very good job on that, baby."

Thank you, Mama.

I didn't get paid for the song or the sessions, but it didn't matter to me because for the first time in my life I felt like a million bucks. Next time we got together, Lummie bought us some hot dogs in exchange for our time. I could dig it. We all knew he was working on the come, meaning if we had a hit, then he'd get his money and

we'd get ours. Either way it was okay with me, because I felt that no matter what, somehow my true life's journey had finally begun.

Not that there weren't some bumps in the road. I was still trying to learn how to control that hot temper still gurgling inside of me just below the surface. I remember one night during a session with the group, there was this white engineer who seemed to me to be very disrespectful. He was one of those types who thought he had to holler at everyone to get things done. At one point, from inside the booth, he turned to me out on the floor and said, "Hey, what the fuck are you doing?"

I was no one to lay that kind of attitude on. He would have been better off to leave those kinds of words alone when he was talking to me. I didn't know the mike was open. I turned to the other guys and said, angrily, "Who does this cat think he is?" That's when they all got quiet and defensive. They knew where I was coming from and didn't want to see any of my street attitude in a place where we were trying to make music. At that moment, I burst through the door to the control room and grabbed the engineer. Just then this little, older white man off in the corner waved me over and said in a soft voice, "What's your name, young man?"

I said, "Barry White."

"Mr. White, can I talk to you for a minute?"

We went outside to the hallway. "You seem like a very talented fellow, so let me share something with you that I've learned being in this business as many years as I have. Don't ever talk to people like that in the music business as long as you live. Everything you've worked for will disappear like it never existed. If you get that kind of reputation, you'll never be seen as anything but one more hostile black musician and it'll end for you."

It was a valuable reminder about my earliest lessons regarding attitude, with a few refinements. What works on the street may not work on the inside. Confidence doesn't always mean muscle. Ability isn't enough; the willingness to work with people at the highest level you can must be there as well. On the street, everything, in every sense, was black and white. Here, in the studio, where the operative function was *listening*, everything took on different shades of gray, as in matter. People got along because of their ability and attitude, not their menace. Hearing this advice from a stranger, I promised myself I would never forget it. From that night on, my visible temper evaporated, and the name Barry White gradually came to be associated with a musician who was soft-spoken, polite, and, beyond that, musically talented.

I went to the studio every day and eventually got a chance to play a little keyboard. Now I became the cat who could sing *and* play, one of the few my age who could do both. I was a rhythm pianist who took his cue from the rhythms of life. That became my thing, what I started to become known for among other musicians. What it meant was that I took that natural rhythm I had already incorporated into the way I walked and the way I talked into the way I played. Other musicians kept telling me I was good, and my name started to get around in studio circles. People began talking about me. "Hey, have you heard this new guy Barry White? He has this certain style of playing . . ."

I branched out and began working with several different local groups. I did a little singing with the Atlantics and some with the Majestics, while continuing with the Upfronts, gradually becoming more directly involved in the producing end of recording our songs onto records.

THAT SEPTEMBER, my probation came to an end. I was in the twelfth grade, and, because I'd spent all that time in Juvey, still four months away from graduating. But one day I made a decision to take advantage of my growing reputation on the local music scene. I decided on the morning of my seventeenth birthday to quit school and go to Hollywood.

I never really liked school all that much anyway, mostly because I was never able to stay at one long enough to feel a part of any program. One I did love was 20th Street Grammar, where I went through the sixth grade. I learned a lot during those years, until we had to move when Mama couldn't pay the rent.

The next school I went to was 28th Street Grammar. I had a teacher there I really liked, Mr. Kelly. He was thin, black, and reminded me of Robert Taylor. All the kids loved him. He was real and didn't take any garbage from anybody.

After that I attended John Adams Junior High for a semester. I had another great teacher there for homeroom, Mr. McCombs. He was a very dignified man, the first one I'd see in the morning after arriving at the school. I liked his little neat mustache, the way he dressed, the way he talked. He acted like a father to all the boys in the class, and I could get into that as well.

Another teacher, Miss Emerson, from the ninth grade, had a certain style and grace and was always kind and understanding to me. I remember one day in junior high she ran down the entire roster of the class, telling everybody who was going to make it in life and who wasn't. I had never heard anything like that from a teacher before. She said, "Some of you who haven't necessarily done as well as some of the others with higher grades are going to achieve more than anybody else, starting with young Mr. Barry White."

I couldn't believe it! I had no clue that she understood anything about me. She must have sensed that early desire on my part to want to do something with my life, to make myself better, to escape from the dead-end prison the world of South Central seemed to me. She recognized that in me and it reinforced my own belief in myself. I knew she could teach me a lot more if I could only have stayed in that school long enough to learn and eventually graduate.

But I couldn't. Mama got about sixty dollars a month from the county, for her, Darryl, and me to live on, and it just wasn't enough. It made me not want to give my full attention to anything that went on in the classroom because I knew if I put too much into it, sooner or later I'd be disappointed when we'd have to move. I'd have to change schools, I'd lose all my old friends, and be forced to deal with new and strange places with kids I didn't know and who didn't know me.

What made this even more difficult for me at John Adams were the connections I had, not only with my teachers, but with some of my schoolmates as well as with music and dancing. I can still remember going with the other kids to a nearby corner hot dog counter that had a jukebox. It's where I heard Bo Diddley for the first time. I couldn't believe the sound he put on record! We used to dance to him every day, sometimes for the entire lunchtime, playing one song over and over again: "Bo Diddley." I quickly got a cold reputation for being the best dancer in school. Both my parents were terrific dancers, and I guess I got my skills from them. My dancing made me a girl magnet. I had that great sense of rhythm, and every little girly around knew it. I was so good at school that when they were asked to supply a dancer for the citywide May Day Pageant, I was the one they chose.

Still, the idea of leaving school had been coming for a long time, and that morning my probation ended, as soon as I opened my eyes I knew I wasn't going back.

It's Now or Never.

It had come to me just like that. The hardest part was having to tell my mother I was quitting. That wasn't going to be easy.

"Why, Barry, why, when you're so close to finishing?" she said after I let her know. She sobbed through a choked voice I can still hear to this day. I never heard my mama cry like that before.

"Because, Mama, I'm going to Hollywood."

There was no other way to explain it. I just knew it was time to make my own place in this world. To do so, I had to learn what went on in Hollywood. I'd heard good things about the place, and bad things as well. Either way, I knew that Hollywood was where the big boys in the music business were, and I wanted to see it for myself.

I got dressed while my mother was still weeping like it was the end of the world, begging me not to. "You don't know nobody, you have no money, you have no clothes, you have no car . . . you're a young black boy going out into a grown-up white world, Barry."

"I know, Mama," I said, quietly but with conviction. "You're right. I may be messing myself up. I'm not going to finish school. I have no money, no car, no clothes, and no connections. I don't know anybody . . . *and I'm black!*" Everything and everybody that could possibly be against me was. Except for one person—me.

"I don't have none of those tools, Mama, but I do have something you didn't mention. Something you yourself taught me. I've got *determination,* Mama! That's why I've *got* to go to Hollywood."

S U R E   E N O U G H, later that same day I found myself standing at the fabled cross-streets of Hollywood and Vine. I saw people everywhere, rushing along their way. Some were driving shiny new cars, and I wondered how come they had no dents in them. There were well-dressed people everywhere walking along the street smiling and saying nice things to each other. "Hey, how you doing," one of them said to me as he passed. I couldn't believe it. Another said, "Have a nice day" and meant nothing more than *to wish me a nice day.* That was when and where I first discovered that everybody wasn't automatically the same, that there really were nice people out there, black and white. It was a revelation to me because I'd been raised where everybody had an attitude and gang-bangers were mean-spirited dudes who never trusted strangers or did *anything* just to be nice.

I walked a couple of streets along the boulevard, looked up, and saw the famous spindle-shaped Capitol Records building. I'd heard about it and seen it on TV, but standing right here in front of it, that was a whole other thing. I passed by the famed Wallich's Music City record and appliance store. In their window were some of the coldest stereo components I could ever have imagined.

I made this journey every morning, and one day I happened to run into a friend of mine I knew from the 'hood who invited me to sit in on a nearby recording session at Leon Renee's studio. Together we walked the few blocks south of the main drag. Leon owned a label called Class Records that featured some really good singers. Eugene Church recorded for Class, so did Bobby Day, who had a big two-sided hit record, "Rockin' Robin" and "Over and Over."

When we got there I decided to introduce myself to Leon. That's when I noticed Guggee Renee, a really *bad* organ player I knew from the 'hood. Guggee and three girls were working on a tune they called "Tossin' Ice Cubes." I didn't think much of the song, but midway through, it turned out Leon needed a syncopation hand clap to lay on the track. He tried three different union players, not one of whom could snag it.

That rhythm thing again, so *deceptively* hard for most people. It was getting late and Leon was about to give it up when I said quietly to my friend, "I can do that." My mother always told me my voice had a way of carrying, and sure enough, my words reached all the way across the room to Leon.

He looked at me, for the first time really, and said, "Hey, who are *you?*"

"Barry White."

"Barry White," he said slowly, as if measuring me up. "And you say you can clap your hands to this rhythm?"

"I sure can."

He told me to come into the recording booth, played the track again, and I nailed that clap in one take. Leon was amazed at first, then ecstatic. The session was only paying union scale, about twenty-five dollars, but he was so happy he gave me a hundred-dollar bill as he shook my hand and said, "You nailed it, son. Thank you. What's your name again?"

"Barry White."

"Well, Barry White, I think you're a very gifted man." The sound in his voice added a layer of meaning to his words that instilled a newborn sense of confidence in me. It was like he was saying "I don't know you, I never heard of you, but you're a real talent." He kept looking in a way that encouraged me more than getting the hand clap right and more than the hundred dollars. That look was the passkey to my future.

I had earned real money without having to look over my shoulder for the police while doing it! A hundred dollars free and clear of what we used to call the *police tax!*

I walked out of the studio, onto a side street near Hollywood Boulevard, made a left, and there on the corner of Selma and Vine found a little hot dog stand. I was feeling so proud I decided to treat myself! I smiled and looked around. Hey, man, I thought, at least one person in this town knows my name. When Mr. Renee handed me that hundred dollars, he'd made me a legitimate working member of the music capital of the world—Hollywood, USA!

I finished my dog, threw the napkin into the trash, and for a second forgot exactly where I was. I had ninety-nine dollars in my fist and some change in my pocket and felt completely lost, until I realized I was truly *found.* I decided to walk home because I didn't want to spend another dime of that money. I wanted to give it all to my mother. I wanted to prove to her that I'd been right, that I could do something worthwhile by *going to Hollywood.*

So I returned by foot, via the identical three-and-a-half-hour route I'd used to get there, but with one big difference. Walking to Hollywood that morning I was just one more dreamer pounding the pavement. Going home that afternoon as a working musician, *I was walking on air.*

THREE

ON MY WAY

"I'VE FOUND SOMEONE"

Never thought I'd find someone
Who drove my mind, girl, like you do.
And never thought I'd see
The day that it could be so true, yeah.
Yes, I've found someone,
Yeah, someone that I can
Give my love to,
And do all the things
I've longed to do.
Girl, I've found out, it's you, it's true,
It's true, it's you.

L ADIES, YOU NOT only have the power to get rid of those bad feelings in your life, but the things that cause them, that bring them on. The truth is, you can literally throw those feelings out of your mind. My mother used to say to me when I was a little boy, "You have a choice in life, to be happy or angry. Please be happy as a gift to yourself." It is indeed a gift and I want to pass it along to you. It is your choice in life to be happy. It is your choice in life to choose someone to love and to love the one you've chosen. Just be a little careful, is all. Learn that falling in love may not last forever, it certainly isn't easy to sustain, but your capacity to keep on loving does. We renew our inner feelings as surely and as inevitably as the seasons come and go. Once we love and lose, we always feel we can never love again. When that happens, we make poor choices, or throw our love away foolishly, believing it makes no difference anyway. This is a clear sign that you have temporarily, at least, lost the ability to love yourself. Love has an emotional shape and starts forming within us first. We have to know who we are before we can love ourselves, and then know who it is we want to give that love to. Love is priceless yet everywhere. The ticket to admission into that special place where love lives can be gotten only by feeling you are already there in your heart. Use your power to love wisely, ladies, please, use it wisely, and you will be happy.

As you know by now, the first love of my life was my mother. After wandering in the emotional desert for a while, I found the second. That woman *was Lady Music. The song "I Found Someone" is, on one level, a celebration of her saying yes to my proposal that we be partners in life. I still love her as much today as I did when we first met and still willingly worship at her pedestal. I write to her, about her, for her, and through her about and for womankind. I love her, try to please her, and try to be like her as well. That's how I know I can relate to both sides of my creative soul, the masculine and the feminine, because when you love someone, you have to love them completely, don't you? I am so completely devoted to her, which is why she has never let me down. It took me eleven and a half years to earn the privilege of touching her beautiful face. I've learned to respect her beyond any woman. Everybody wants her, I know. But I love her in a special way. We've been fruitful and had lots of babies together. Every song, every album is the product of our love. Yes, baby . . . I know . . . I love you and thank you for marrying my soul to yours.*

Whether it's your art or your woman, the conditions of love remain the same. Love your special other the way I love my lady music, and you will find a level of happiness you never knew was possible.

• • •

IN 1962, NOT LONG after that first session at Leon Renee's studio, I started getting calls for more session work. Word had gotten around about me being this dude with a good sense of rhythm. I kept my eyes and ears open, and took it all in. In a way it was like being back in school, only this was a classroom that made perfect sense to me. These weren't lessons that were put out there for a group of kids who sat daydreaming as they waited for the bell to ring. This was an excursion into learning where music in its component parts—rhythm and melody—*spoke to me.*

I got calls from the oddest places, at least as far as I was concerned. When white surfer bands wanted me to help them produce their records, I was there ready to go. I cut seven different white acts during this period, which was highly unusual because, as the Hollywood-based recordings in those days reflect, very few black people in those days interacted with whites in the studio. I could never understand this. I didn't want to know

about the politics, or the business, or the barriers. To me, if I couldn't work with whites when I had the opportunity, I would consider myself only half a talent.

I happened to be in the studio one day when I started noticing this guy they all were calling the writer. I heard someone say "we need a rewrite" and I thought to myself, "What the hell is a rewrite?" I decided to ask one of the other musicians.

"Well," he said, "that's when they want you to redo the lyrics, to change them, to make it stronger here, stronger there . . ."

"Is that all he does? And he gets paid for it?"

"He sure does, man."

I was accumulating all this key information, you see, like I said, and a lot of it was coming from white people. I guess there weren't a lot of brothers in L.A. with a lot of knowledge of rewriting, or unions, or dealing with publishers, or setting up studio sessions, all of that end of making records. I was different; I wanted to learn everything I could about the process, from anywhere and anyone. It didn't make any difference to me what color they were.

One day a few weeks later, while sitting at home in Mama's chair by myself, thinking about all the new things I was learning, I began to realize that if I tried really hard, I just might actually be able to make a pretty good living at this music thing.

Then, as if on cue, I heard the *Voice.*

You know, Barry, you could probably write, arrange, and produce a record all on your own. . . .

That was the moment I dedicated myself to accomplishing just that. For the next four months, I intensified my self-training and used every contact I knew to try to put it together.

However, in spite of all my focus, energy, and determination, by the summertime, the phone had stopped ringing.

At first I thought maybe I had done or said something wrong to somebody. I couldn't understand why no one was calling for my services anymore. So here was the next lesson from the school of Real Life. *In the music business steady jobs, and therefore regular paychecks, are never guaranteed.* And because I didn't have enough knowledge and experience, I did the worst possible thing I could—I started to question my own abilities. I had to overcome a lot of self-doubt before I was able to realize that no matter who you are, no matter how good you can be, you're going to hit on some days and miss on others. What you have to hope is you don't miss too many days and eat up the bread you make on the days you do get work. I was determined to keep myself on the plus side of that equation.

Still, as '62 slid into '63, I didn't as yet have a decent enough grip on this business they call music. I tried to write a couple of songs by myself and discovered that my talents weren't as fully developed as I'd hoped. Truthfully, the first lyrics I attempted on my own were pretty awful. Pitiful even. I rhymed everything and used way too many words to try to say what I wanted to say. However, the first *music* I wrote, that's another story. I finished my first piece in 1963, and although I wouldn't get a chance to record it for ten more years, I knew it was good. I called it "Love's Theme." I'm thrilled to say that today it's become an anthem, having sold more than 4 million copies and hit the charts three different times. BMI recently gave me an award when the song passed the three *million* mark in airplay. *Wide World of Sports* helped that cause when it used "Love's Theme" on its Saturday afternoon golf program for sixteen years.

But as I say, that kind of success was a long time coming. In 1963 things got so bad I began to have serious doubts about whether I could stay in the music business at all. My number one problem was trying to figure out how to make money more consistently. I was stone broke, which meant I had to find a so-called real job. That was a drag because if there was one thing I hated to do then and still do to this day, it's get up early to go to work. Not that I couldn't do it. When I had to, when we needed the bread, I was willing to work at all kinds of odd jobs.

From an early age, I understood this kind of responsibility. When I was just eight, Mama said that because I was the oldest "man" in the family, she was putting me in charge of our modest insurance policies.

"Why are you giving these to me now?" I asked her.

"Because you're the more solid of my two boys. If something happens to Mama, I want you to know where everything is."

"More solid" was Mama's way of saying that Darryl was too busy to take care of things at home because he was intent on making a career out of robbing people. Oh, yes, my mother knew what he was up to but was powerless to stop him. It affected her so deeply she began having terrible dreams about Darryl. One Thursday night she dreamed he was in a terrible fight with a cat, got all scratched up, and nearly died. The next morning at breakfast she said to him, "Baby, why don't you skip going out tonight?"

He didn't but I did. By then I was mostly off the streets and preferred staying home. I no longer needed gangs or any of the other stuff that so consumed Darryl. My only real passion then was music.

So there I was, alone in the room, happily playing 45s on my blue and white portable record player. I was always trying to figure out what all the different labels meant, who was singing on what song, how this sound on that record matched that sound on this one.

Suddenly Darryl burst through the front door, headed straight for the bathroom. At first I didn't pay any attention to the noise he made as he pushed his way through the living room. My back was to him, so I couldn't see he was holding the right side of his face down like a flap, to keep blood from squirting out of it like water from a fountain. I followed him to the bathroom. He turned around and that was the first time I saw he was completely soaked in blood.

I'd never seen that much blood in my life. I threw my arms around him and held him as tears filled my eyes. I kept telling him over and over he was going to be all right. Just then my mother, who had been at some church function, came home. When she saw Darryl, the first thing she blurted out was, "Didn't I tell you not to go out tonight?" She tried but couldn't stop the bleeding. She wrapped his head in a towel and took him to the hospital, where they had to stitch him up from his ear to his neck.

He barely survived that incident but was soon busted for hitting a bank and kidnapping some women he and his crew threw out of their speeding car and onto the freeway. As I stood there that day, a dark chill raced down my spine. If I wasn't careful to follow the right path, if I didn't keep absolutely on top of things in my life, I could easily be watching my own future being played out before me. I needed to anchor myself in a way that would, if nothing else, impose a sense of responsibility that would keep my head on my shoulders, my mind on my music, and my bank book on the plus side.

That's one of the reasons why, when I turned eighteen, I welcomed more responsibilities as a way to prove I was a decent, honest guy. The other reason was that at this time I became not only the big man of my mama's house but the head of another as well when I finally married Mary.

I hadn't seen her for awhile, ever since that day with Clifton. I even found another girlfriend when I got out of jail. However, one night I was at a party, Mary was there, we started talking about the one child we'd already had and the other still on the way. The next thing I knew, we were back together.

It was after she gave birth to our second child, Lanece (Nese), that Mary and her mother pushed me hard to get married.

I was a different person from the one who'd gone a little crazy and spent time in jail. For one thing, I stopped drinking, and for another, I got married. The ceremony took place November 18, 1963. I have to say that with all our mutual pledges of love, I still had serious doubts about the wisdom of this move. Besides the fact that my feelings had changed, I felt too young and incapable of being the man of my own house. In spite of my size and streetwise sensibilities, I was very much still a baby myself. I figured there was no way I could handle fatherhood. Anyway, I was the only one Mama had left at home to take care of her, and I had nothing like any kind of a real music career and therefore no steady income going for myself.

Why then did I go through with it, when I knew we were both too young to get married and I was unsure about my feelings? After Nese was born, Mary's mother kicked my ass as hard as she could until we made our relationship legal and our children legitimate. The result was that after avoiding it for as long as I could, I did what I thought was the right thing and walked down the aisle in front of the proverbial shotgun.

AS SOON AS we got through at the church, Mary went back to her house and I went back to mine. I didn't want her staying with me. I didn't even want anyone to know that I had gotten married. Mary, of course, wanted *everyone* to know. That's why I made her go home with her parents. We lived like that for the first six months of our marriage, while my mama tried to convince me how wrong it was. "She's your *wife* now," she kept telling me. "She belongs with you."

"I know, Mama," I told her, "but the truth is, I don't really *like* her all that much anymore." Which was true. Marriage and babies had somehow taken the fun out of everything for me. I really had no idea what I'd gotten myself into. Even though I felt totally unprepared, I realized I had to face the inevitable, do what everybody kept saying was the right thing and find an apartment for us.

By the time I turned twenty we were the parents of *two* small children, Barry, Jr., and Nese. As far as I was concerned, I was just another kid in the house, even if I was the head of it. I couldn't wait for mine to be old enough to play hide and go seek with me. Two more years passed and that meant two more children for us—Nina and Darryl. This was how I'd wanted it—a boy at the beginning, two daughters in between, and a boy at the end to protect them.

I was now a family man with no job and *no money.* I struggled mightily to take care of my family, to protect and provide for them. A friend of mine suggested I might have an easier time if I just left my wife and children, that my chances of making it would be so much better because of the freedom I'd then have to travel and take music jobs for little or no pay. I remember when he said that, I turned and told him, "Hey, I'm not leaving my kids for *anything.*" I meant it. I wasn't going to make those little ones pay for my wanting to be in music. I'd brought them into this world, and I was going to care for them, even if it meant never playing another note the rest of my life.

When it came to my kids I never wavered, even though my marriage held nothing for me now except problems. Being in the studio, writing a song, working with artists, that is where I wanted to be and what I wanted to be doing. Those sentiments never sat all that well with Mary. As far as she was concerned, my first and *only* priority was to provide for her and the kids, even though before we'd gotten married she knew I was in the Upfronts and never said anything bad about my wanting to be in the music business. Now, four kids later, she was singing a different tune and insisted I get a "real" job.

My response to her about this was always the same: "Are you married now?"

"Yes."

"Well, you got what you wanted, why shouldn't I get what I want? I'll be the best father anyone has ever seen to our kids, but I still have to do my thing, Mary."

Her mama always took her side in this, which just made everything more difficult for me.

To keep peace in the family and bread on the table, I tried the eight-to-five gig. I worked in a car wash, I cut and processed hair, I did house painting. I got some work at the county general hospital, although that job proved far too creepy. One day I was working near the laundry drop chute where a lot of trash would come down and there was a white brother standing next to me. He was a little too close to the chute and suddenly found himself covered from head to toe with bloody used surgical linen. The next thing he knew the doctors and nurses were all over him, sticking him with antibiotics like he was a pincushion. That scared me.

Another time I was working in the morgue and one cadaver just all of a sudden seemed to sit up and *talk to me!* This nearly frightened me out of my skin. He sounded like he was very much alive. What I didn't know was dead bodies often have air in their lungs and that when you move them they pass gas and make a noise through their throats for the last time. The force of that gas can also make them "move."

I also got a job doing construction on the sports arena in downtown L.A., only a block from one of the places where I lived as a kid, never dreaming that one day I would be riding to it in a limo for a sold-out concert, go down the parking ramp, look up, see my name in lights on the billboard, and the very same blue roof I'd helped put up to hold together the walls between which twenty thousand of my fans now awaited my arrival.

Unfortunately for me, that day was still a long way off. At this stage of my life and career, there never seemed to be enough money for everyone to eat, let alone for me to dream. I always made sure the family was fed first, and then, if we ran out of food, I'd go to the supermarket and start filling up a cart with items like bread, cereal, and canned foods. When I'd get to the back where they kept the roasted chickens, I'd put a couple in my wagon and while I walked the rest of the aisles I'd eat them. After I finished, I'd leave the cart filled with groceries and walk out. Some might call it stealing. I call it survival.

Marriage did teach me some valuable lessons, among them being how sacred that institution is. When it's right, the honeymoon should never end and the drudgery should never begin. Once the commitment is made to share your life, it needs to be real and total. You need to share your dreams as well, so when the opportunity to live them comes along you're ready and able to go for it and take the person you love along for the grand ride. While I was still with Mary, I knew early on she wasn't that person. Something did happen though, in its own way, that helped push me closer to where I knew I really wanted to be and who I knew I really was.

It began one Tuesday morning in 1964 when there was a knock at my door. Strangers who come knocking at ghetto doors usually have a briefcase, a holster, and a badge. One way or the other it's usually bad news.

"Who is it?" I asked through the door.

A voice came back at me. "Al Samuels."

Now who the hell is Al Samuels? I asked myself. I automatically reverted to that defensive mode, braced myself, and opened the door.

"Are you Barry White?"

"Yes," I said, scoping him. He was white. He looked for all the world like The Man to me, but I wasn't scared because I knew I hadn't done anything wrong.

"Can I come in and talk to you for a minute?"

He didn't look very threatening, so I invited him in. He took a kitchen chair, got comfortable, looked at me, and said, "Mr. White, I want to open a toy store in this neighborhood. I've been trying to find a guy who can really take care of himself and my operation as well. Everyone I ask mentions your name. I thought I'd come by, introduce myself to you, and see about the possibility of our doing some business."

"What would you want me to do?"

"Come to my store and I'll teach you how to sell toys."

Sell toys? That's about as far away from music as you can get!

"I can't pay you a regular salary," he said, "but I will give you some money to get by on every now and then."

He went on to tell me that if I built up the business with him, one day he'd give me a piece of it. I'd never had any kind of offer like that in my life. I thought about it and there didn't seem to be any downside. What did I have to lose? The record business wasn't doing anything for me at the moment, and at least this gig would keep me close to home. The location he'd picked out for his store was right there in South Central L.A., just around the corner from where I was living. If nothing else it meant I could walk to work.

The next day he showed me the building he wanted to rent, on Santa Barbara Boulevard (before it was changed to Martin Luther King, Jr.

Boulevard). He took me inside and pointed out where he was going to hang his pegboard, the stuff you put the hooks into to hang up the toys. I honestly didn't have any idea what he was talking about.

Then he said, "I'm going to take you downtown and show you where to buy toys wholesale. I want you to pay attention and watch what I do."

"They got a lot of toys down there?"

"They've got nothing but toys."

SO I NOW DEVOTED MYSELF to learning the business of running a retail toy store. I worked eighteen hours a day every day, because I knew that, like with my music, if I made a commitment, it had to be total. It was important to me that people knew whoever they were and whatever they did, when they got Barry White, they got devotion, honesty, and integrity.

The first time we went downtown to buy our merchandise I was blown away. I'd never seen that many toys in my life! Expensive toys, cheap toys, all the toys I'd seen since I was a kid were here in this single, huge wholesale warehouse. I never knew anything about warehousing, or the business of buying and selling merchandise of any kind. Standing in that warehouse I fell in love with the whole idea of selling toys, and thought that maybe this was the direction I should go in my life.

Mr. Samuels could sense my enthusiasm and suggested we buy toys with lots of color, toys that did things, mechanical toys, trucks that went *mmmmmmffff!* Before too long I became good enough to be a buyer. I went to the warehouse every Tuesday and Friday, and sometimes Thursday if my inventory was running low. Mr. Samuels kept telling me I couldn't sell what I didn't have. I decided to take the initiative. I ran sales in the store, sales he sometimes wasn't even aware of. I gave away a lot of merchandise, which developed a great ongoing relationship with the parents and children. I knew I must be doing a pretty good job because one day a teacher who worked with grammar school kids came by the store talking about how remarkably I was doing. "The kids really like you," she told me. "They think you're so cool! They talk about you and can't wait to get out of school so they can come to your store."

I worked all day, every day, and after we closed, from six to eleven every night when I moved the toys around so no one item of merchandise was ever in the same place. Nobody told me to do this, but I knew that every day the kids came in, it should look like a brand-new store to them, and they saw things they never saw before. And that made them want to come back every day. One time this kid, about ten years old, came in to get this big fire engine truck, and his little brother, who was about a quarter his size, stuck a penny up on the counter and looked at me like he was waiting on his fire engine too. He didn't have to wait very long. I just reached up and gave him one.

IT DIDN'T TAKE very long before we were doing so much business that Kresse's, our main competition down on Central, went out of business. Mr. Samuels then took me aside and said, "We have to get a bigger store, Barry, because you're really kicking ass in this town." Over and over he told me how well I was doing and even showed me the receipts to prove the business I was generating. That was a proud moment in my life.

I trusted Al completely. He wanted to see me be successful. One day he came back to my house. He knew from his first visit we didn't have much in the way of furniture and said, "I want you to get some things for your home."

"What do you mean?"

He said, "You need a couch, a bed, bunk beds for your kids, and some appliances."

"Al, are you sure we can afford this?"

"We can afford it, Barry."

So the next day I went down to Gold's Furniture Store on Washington and Central, a place where I'd always wanted to shop, where every black person who lived in the neighborhood and had money bought their furniture. I didn't go crazy—after all, Mr. Samuels was nice enough to want to help me—but the first thing I picked out was something I'd always wanted: a stereo set. Even though I was no longer going to Hollywood every day, I was still in love with music and felt that I'd never really left it. So I got a stereo, along with a couch and chair, and bunk beds for the kids. My children had been sleeping on mattresses on the floor. Now I could give another family in the neighborhood those mattresses. I also bought a big bed to sleep in. The last thing I picked out was a stove, and called it a day.

When Mr. Samuels saw what I'd bought, the first thing he said was, "That's all?"

"This is all I need, Al. Just enough to get me by for now."

He looked at me and smiled.

The next morning the delivery truck pulled up to my house. When the neighbors came out and saw this big, heavy truck from Gold's, I knew what they were thinking. "Why are they going to Barry White's house?" They pulled the shipping blankets off the stuff, and now everybody saw my new things. I didn't like this, but I couldn't stop it. Because I'd never bought furniture before I didn't know that's the program, or I would have told them to leave the blankets on until they were in the house.

There was still an element of burglary in this neighborhood, and you couldn't be flashing your goods. The other part of it was that for the store, this was a form of marketing, to let another black family see what this one was getting, to make them want to go down to Gold's themselves.

The neighbors seemed genuinely happy for me, and a couple of sisters were even crying. "Oh, Barry, you deserve it, the toy store must really be doing good . . ."

"Yeah," I said, "not bad."

Two days later the truck pulled back up to my house and the men took all the stuff back. The check that Al had written for the furniture bounced. I couldn't understand how that happened, since we were supposed to be doing so well. I began to wonder if Al was cheating on the business, which meant he was cheating on me. The same neighbors who'd watched the furniture being brought in now watched it being taken away. And that's not all. I'd already given away my old stuff to the other families. What a mess! I had no idea what to do next, except I knew I had to do it fast.

After they took the furniture, I went down to the toy store. When Al came in that evening he couldn't tell anything was wrong, because I'm not a person who shows hurt. Instead, I sucked it up.

"How you doing, Barry?" he said.

"Oh, fine, Al. What's new today on the agenda?"

"Well, there's some new toys coming out Monday. If you go to the wholesaler on Tuesday they'll probably be there."

"Okay."

It wasn't until later on that day that he asked me in a casual fashion how the furniture was working out.

"Oh," I said, "they came and got it this morning, Al."

"Really? I wonder why?"

I could tell he knew he'd fucked up, but I played along. "There's something about the check. If you call them they'll tell you why."

Now he tried to play like they'd made a mistake. "But don't worry, Barry. I'll straighten it out."

He never did get me back my furniture, but I didn't hold it against him. I kept working like nothing happened, trying to survive the best way I could, mainly because I so desperately needed the money. Al started giving me an extra fifty dollars here, seventy-five dollars there, which I used to buy some cheap used furniture. One day not long after, he started talking big again. "We gotta get a new building, Barry, a bigger place."

When he found the location he liked just up the street we moved everything there, which took me and Bernie, a neighborhood friend of mine I'd gotten a job helping out in the store, one whole night. Al wanted us to do it that way so we wouldn't miss a single day's business. That's what he wanted, that's what I gave him. The next day when he arrived to open, he couldn't believe it. Everything was up and ready to go.

About two months later, he said he had the feeling we were doing *too* good. Somebody was checking us out, he insisted, probably to rip us off. He rented a little room in a motel across the street and planted Bernie and me in it to sit up and watch the store all night. He also got each of us a gun. Another slick move, I thought to myself. This dude was always so eager to put everything on my big shoulders and then ride atop them once the trouble passed. Now he was putting murder on me. He wasn't about to shoot anybody, no sir, but it was okay if I did it. I got a creeping feeling down my spine that I was somehow being sucked right back down into the South Central whirlwind that led straight to nowhere, the one I'd fought so hard to pull myself out of.

Fortunately for everybody, no one ever showed up, nothing happened to the store, and no one got into any more trouble. No one, that is, except Al Samuels, because one day not long after my last all-night spying gig, I came in the next morning and the store was completely empty. All the toys were gone, the pegboards, even the pegs, and there was no Al to be found anywhere.

I stood in the center of the huge empty space and cried my eyes out. This hurt me more than what happened with the furniture, more, really, than anything before in my life. I kept crying until it came to me that I had really messed things up myself. I had trusted Al Samuels, a total stranger. I should have had some sort of a formal agreement with him. I should have done a lot of things. I learned a hard but valuable lesson that day. No matter how much you want to, in this life, in this world, you simply cannot trust everybody. You have to learn to pick who you can and who you can't.

As for Al, he was either very brave or very stupid, because without my knowing it, he'd gotten himself still another place, over on Hoover and 42nd, right in my old neighborhood. Three weeks later he actually came *back* to the house and offered Mama, who lived upstairs, my old job! She listened politely before telling him she'd think it over. When he left and I came home, she told me what happened and blew her top. "The nerve of that man! He's offered me your job! He messed you up and now he wants to mess me up."

It surprised her when I said, "Mama, *we need the money.* If you want to take the job you should. I guarantee he will never misuse you." In the ghetto, you understand, mothers are sacred. You can mess with a guy but never with his family, and *especially* not with his mother. If you do, you're taking something to another, very bad, place. I didn't think Al was that stupid.

Meanwhile, Mama was cussin' and talkin' bad. This was the first time I'd ever heard her say something bad about another person. When she finished, I said, "So when do you start work, Mama?"

"Start work? I'm not workin' for that man."

"Yes you are. We need the money, Mama."

"You mean you still want me to go to work for that bastard, after he's ripped you off and all?"

"I sure do. I want you to go over there with a smile. I want you to be the best employee his money can buy. It's a chance for us that we have to take."

So she did it, she went to work for him, and in fairness, I have to say that Al took very good care of my mother. I thought maybe this was his way of trying to pay me back.

Now, Al Samuels was a lucky man. A *very* lucky man. He didn't *know* how lucky he was. After my mother started working for him, Darryl got released from a twenty-two-month stint in state prison and was free. First thing he heard when he got back on the street was about how this white guy by the name of Al Samuels had screwed his brother and was now trying to mess with his mama.

I was home, and it was one of those brief periods of time I was able to afford to keep a phone in service, which is how I got the call from Mama at the store. "Barry, you gotta come over right now. Your brother's here and he's going to kill Al."

I put the phone down and ran as fast as I could. When I got to the store, the first thing I heard was Al Samuels's voice coming from the back, pleading for his life. "Please don't kill me. Please, I didn't mean to hurt your brother, I didn't mean . . . I had no plans to hurt your mother . . . Darryl, please, she's the greatest employee I ever had . . ."

I came up behind and heard Darryl say, "That's bullshit, man, my brother was the greatest worker you ever had. He got you enough money so you could move over there from Santa Barbara to here, *motherfucker!*"

"Burly . . ." When we said it to each other those days, it was like pulling the attention trigger. It meant you had to stop messing around and really listen.

Darryl had Al up in his collar and was holding a fire ax in one hand, ready to cut the man's head off. He turned to me and said, "I was gonna bring his head to you, Burly." I told you, Darryl was one cold-blooded dude.

I said, "Burly, you just out the joint, man. This guy ain't worth killing. All he done is cheated me out a few dollars. It's a little business, it ain't worth it. I ain't pissed off and saying go on and kill him, now, am I? Besides, he's taking good care of Mama, he brings her home every day, she never has to catch a bus or nothin' . . ."

"No," Darryl said, "this *motherfucker* got to go. There can't be no white *motherfucker* come into our family and do this, man." Darryl was looking at Al with those killer eyes of his, set back up in his head, his eyebrows hanging over. I had to make my move or Al was dead. Darryl was a big boy, like me, and although I would never have wanted to tangle with him, I knew how to handle him in a situation like this. I simply put my long arms around Darryl's chest, picked him up off the ground, and carried him four blocks down the street, even as he was fighting to get loose. "No, Burly, let me go, let me fuck him up . . ."

"I can't let you," I said, holding him in my arms. "You ain't doin' it and goin' back to jail . . ."

It took awhile, Burly stayed pissed for a long time, but finally later that night he got to a point where I could at least reason with him and got him to promise to leave Al alone. It was real late when I finally got into my bed, exhausted from all that had gone down.

And that was when the Voice finally returned. This time it said, very plaintively, *"How'd you like your ass whippin'?"* I sat up in the dark, my wife lyin' next to me asleep. I said softly, "What do you mean how'd I like my ass whippin' . . ."

The next time you do what you did it's going to be worse than what happened tonight.

"The next time?"

"Yes! The next time you leave music! Eleven months is long enough to be fuckin' around with this toy shit. It's time to get your ass back into the journey."

It couldn't have been any clearer than that. I got the message and right then and there vowed never to leave music again, no matter what.

MORE CHANGES CAME QUICKLY after that, beginning with Darryl and ending with the final breakup of my marriage.

Darryl had gotten into some more serious trouble and was hit with an indefinite sentence of nothing to fifty. I wouldn't see my brother outside again for thirteen and a half years, until 1978, when he'd eventually be released because the sentence was declared unconstitutional. When he went away, I felt a part of myself had been taken that I wouldn't get back for a long, long time. It made both my mother and me very sad, and I didn't know what to do to make it better for either of us.

As for Mary, seven years of marriage had turned her into one big complaint machine, and now she had my father as well as her mother on her side. He'd become closely involved with my family, often bringing food and sometimes money over to the house, knowing I wasn't working all that much. Occasionally he'd drop hints about how tough it was to crack the music business and how I might want to think about doing something else. I always listened, shook my head, and said the same thing—that I wasn't quite ready to give it all up.

On one of his weekly visits to our home, he said he wanted to have a little talk with me. "Barry," he said, "you're never going to make it in music. You've been trying for so long to make it in this business and you still ain't did shit. One day you're going to look around and the world is going to hit you like a brick in the face. You better think about doing something more constructive."

When he finished, I just thought softly to myself, You know, Daddy, you could be right. I'll see you next week. Oh, and by the way, Daddy, what you just said don't mean shit to me. It isn't what you think about me that matters. It's what *I* think about me that counts.

On Easter Sunday 1969, I came home from some nowhere job I was working. It was about six in the evening. I found Mary in the kitchen. She gave me a kiss and asked if I'd take a little walk with her. Outside, down the street, she turned to me and said she wanted a divorce. Just like that. "You're the only person besides your mother who likes your music. I don't think you're going to make it. You've been at it for almost ten years now and *nothing's happened.* You can't even make enough money to support your own family."

That little speech messed up my head big time. I didn't argue, but inside I felt awful. From the beginning I'd sacrificed everything to give her what she wanted. We agreed that night to continue living together for the sake of the children, and because in reality neither one of us could afford to move out. But there was no mistake about the fact that our marriage was finally officially over. I knew it in my mind, in my heart, in my soul, in my being. I also knew something else. Just about every aspect of my old life was gone, and it was fine with me. I was more than ready for my new life to begin.

As it turned out, I didn't have very long to wait.

FOUR

GUIDED BY DESTINY

"YOU'RE THE FIRST, THE LAST, MY EVERYTHING"

The first, my last, my everything and the answer to all my dreams,
You're my sun, my moon, my guiding star,
My kind of wonderful, that's what you are.
I know there's only, only one like you,
There's no way they could have made two.
You're . . . you're all I'm living for,
Your love I'll keep forever more,
You're the first, you're the last, my everything.

In you I find so many things,
A love so new only you could bring.
Can't you see if you . . . you make me feel this way.
You're like a fresh morning dew
Or a brand new day.

I see so many ways that I
Can love you till the day I die.
You're my reality,
Yet I'm lost in a dream,
You're the first, the last, my everything.

YOU'RE THE FIRST one I'll ever love this way and, of course, the last. That makes you, darling, my everything. I mean that for now and forever. Through the ups, the downs, the good times and the bad. You are my partner through all the days of my life, beside me when I succeed, to share that moment of joy, beside me when I fall, to hold my hand and offer your loyalty and support. You are my muse, and through you I make my music. You are my Lady Music. You are my inspiration. You will always be with me as I make my journey through life. We are together, we are linked. We are all facets of one, our voices united in the harmony of passion. We are the musical essence of romance—the true melody of love unlimited.

Everyone always wants to know what I consider the favorite of all my songs. I'll let you in on a little secret. I have no favorite, because I love them all. They are my children. Could you say you loved one child of yours more than another? You know, each of our children is and has something special and unique. Each is a part of our soul now with a life of his or her own. So too are my songs. They are my children, my messages, and my messengers; they are my life and my love, the innermost part of my soul given to you in the best way I know how. "Love's Theme," "Ecstasy," "Walkin' in the Rain," "You're the First, the Last, My Everything." They all say it best. I love you, baby, Barry White style.

I have always tried to understand and identify with the woman's point of *view. It's one of the things that's made my music so appealing to both men and women. Later on I wrote a song called "I'm So Glad I'm a Woman": "In the morning when I wake up, As I comb my hair, I can hear my daddy saying, It's a big world out there . . ."*

I know there are men out there who will do things to you if you are not careful. As men, we are all fathers to the little girls of this world who grow up to become someone else's girlfriends and wives. We raise them and we love them, we teach them and we protect them. The inner strength of woman is a beautiful thing to watch blossom and take hold. Love brings with it a power and a beauty that complement each other and help create the gorgeous image of our ladies. It is a power and a beauty that is universal, to be sure, and yet each woman we love is an individual, each with her own strengths and unique beauty. In that way they are like the best moments of a beautiful song, where the emotional expression of one's love is a universal declaration, while the time, the place, the circumstance, are completely specific. That is what my music is all about: Everyman's declaration of love for Everywoman, told through one man's love for the singular woman of his life.

• • •

BY 1965 I WAS LONG OVER the misadventures with Al Samuels and his toys and actually starting to get called more frequently to play the occasional session. However, I was still struggling and not making enough to support my family. There were, the last time I counted, 365 days in a year, and I was working nowhere near that amount. What I was accumulating on a very regular basis, though, was a bank of knowledge and connections. Gradually, as people began calling, I discovered it was not always to play on their records. Calls like this: "Hey, Barry, you got a minute?"

"What's happenin' . . ."

"I want you to come by Goldstar Studios and hear something . . ."

I'd go, listen, and tell them what I thought of their recordings. "There's something wrong with this song," I'd say, after giving a careful listening.

"Well, what is it? What does it need?"

"For one thing," I'd say, "you should change that foot bass, take the snare off the four and put it on two and four, and also change the guitar line. Can I talk to your guitar guy?"

"Sure, Barry, talk to him."

I always felt I had the special kind of talent it takes to become an arranger of music. I'd get called to the studio, drop my ideas about what I heard, and two or three months later I'd hear the same song as a hit record on the radio. After that, of course, more phone calls would come in. "Barry, can you come by the studio, I want you to hear something . . ."

That summer I got a phone call from a friend of mine named Jackie Lee—his real name before he changed it to Earle when he was one half of the duo Bob and Earle. They'd had the original hit recording of "Harlem Shuffle," produced by the great Gene Page, whom I had the privilege of meeting during that session.

Of course, I had no way of knowing at the time that one day Gene Page would be the arranger for so many of my own records. He was a great talent and became a very close friend of mine. Because I couldn't read music, he was my unofficial transcriber. In my opinion, he was one of the most educated black men in music. I could always say to him, I want this kind of sound, sing it for him, and he'd be able to put it down as part of the musical arrangement.

After "Harlem Shuffle," the duo floundered and dropped or changed their professional name, something a lot of guys did in those days when they either didn't make it or wanted to start over. That's when Jackie Lee came to me and said, "Hey, Barry, let's write something together . . . let's cut somethin' for ourselves, over in one of them Hollywood studios."

It sounded like a good idea to me. "Okay, Jackie."

The A side of the recording was a tune we came up with called "Ooh Honey Baby." For the B side Jackie wrote something alone called "The Duck." I listened to it once and knew it was going to be a smash. It was a dance novelty, like "The Twist." Normally, I didn't like novelty. There's only been one group that's been able to make a whole career out of it, and that's the Coasters. Still, "The Duck" had hit written all over it.

We released our double-sided single that September, and sure enough, by Christmas "The Duck" had landed us on the charts. Jackie Lee and I were planning our next move, thinking about maybe doing a couple of clubs or something, while I continued to hustle for money to pay the rent.

One night around this time, my cousin Pete came by the house and asked if I'd like to ride with him to take his cousin home.

I had nothing to do so I said okay, and got in his car. We started cruising the neighborhood and just after crossing Figueroa we noticed a street party taking place over to the right. I could tell immediately it was a Businessmen's party. There were so many familiar brothers and sisters there, the action spilled out onto the street. A couple of people shouted out my name when they spotted me in the car. A lot of the brothers from my days in the gang were glad to see me. I'd been off the streets for a while and they wanted to come over to say hello.

So much so, I thought the party was outside. I started to talk to some friends and found out the usual—who was married, who was still single, who was living, who was dead. After a while I got back into the car with Pete when I saw a crowd of brothers swarming around three guys who'd tried to crash the party. You could get killed doing that. I went over to find out who they were and to see if I could help cool this thing out.

Just at that moment, some members of a rival neighborhood gang, the Roman Twenties, showed up to support their friends. The Roman Twenties were the most feared gang in Los Angeles until they were dethroned by the Businessmen. Because we'd done so much moving around as kids, both Darryl and I'd had the unique privilege of, at one time or another, being in *both*.

I could plainly see one of the Businessmen was going to kill one of the Roman Twenties gang-bangers. I walked my way right up to the Roman Twenties' boy and said to him quietly, "Go home, man . . . get out of here and don't you be comin' to parties you ain't invited to."

"Thanks, Barry," he said, scared he might still be given a stage-three-level going-over, and offed. I watched as the other Roman Twenties took him back and left. Everything then seemed to cool down.

What I didn't know was that after I split, one of the three Roman

Twenties crashers, a not-too-bright guy named Milton, had decided to come back to the party. Sure enough, he got messed up, and bad. Someone from the Businessmen shot him at close range, and it didn't look like he was going to make it.

The shooting scattered everyone. Meanwhile, Pete and I dropped off his cousin, and were headed back to my place when, as he barreled down Normandie, we ran smack into a police roadblock.

It was like they were waiting for us. In no time we were surrounded by what seemed like a hundred black-and-whites, officers, and plainclothes detectives. We had no idea what was going down.

"Out of that goddamn car," one of the cops shouted, with his gun drawn. "Put your hands on your heads and get down on the ground!"

They handcuffed us, took us down to the station, and threw us into an interrogation room. A few minutes later three officers came in and stared silently at us. After a long silence, one of them spoke. "Who the hell is Barry White?"

"I am," I said.

"So *you're* the bad boy."

"What's going on?" I asked.

"Oh," one of the cops said to the other with a smirk. "He doesn't know." He looked directly at me. "You'll find out soon enough."

Pete was really nervous now and starting to show it. I was still trying to stay cool as they took us to separate holding cells. It was just eight days before Christmas, and I feared I was about to be locked up, right through the holidays and maybe for a lot longer. I was worried about my kids, and what this would do to my mother.

The next day they took us out of our cells and put us in separate interrogation rooms. Four cops came in to see me. One of them did all the talking. He leaned into me. "So what did you do with the gun?"

I stared right back at him. "What gun?"

"Come on. The one you used over at Figueroa at the Businessmen's party."

"I was only there for a few seconds and nothing happened. I just got in my car and left." That may have not been everything I remembered from the night, but I knew where my loyalties belonged. The police got nobody's names from me, and never would, even if they threatened to lock me up the rest of my life.

"Yeah, well, that's not the way we hear it. The neighbors say everybody was calling your name."

Things now started to become a little clearer. The neighbors never liked it when the gangs put on their street parties. The only name any of the neighbors heard that night was mine, when it was being shouted out by the brothers who came out to the car to greet me. That's how the police knew my name. Because of that, I was going to be charged with shooting Milton. It didn't matter to the police if I was the one who did it. They just cared about getting someone because someone had done it, and to them, all the brothers were the same worthless pieces of shit.

A little while later, as I was lying in the jail for the fifth straight day wondering what was going to happen to me, a voice came over the loud-speaker. He started singing "I'll Be Home for Christmas," then said, "White, roll it up, you're going home." I wasn't sure what I heard. I was still very messed up, because I knew if Milton had died I was looking at Murder One. I thought for sure I was going down.

What I didn't know until I was brought back out was that Milton had been in a coma all those days and the cops had sat at his bedside waiting to interrogate him as to what had happened. Suddenly, miraculously, on the fourth day he came out of it around 3:00 A.M. just long enough to say that Barry White was innocent, *that Barry White was the one who tried to get everyone to stop fighting and to go home!* After clearing me, he slipped back into unconsciousness. But he'd said enough. I was free!

It was the day before Christmas. What a gift! I gladly walked all the way from the jail to my house, telling myself that this was a true miracle, and there must have been a reason for it. Sure enough, in January 1966, "The Duck" reached Number 9 on *Billboard* magazine's R&B chart. Overnight I went from a statistic in a jail cell to a number on the charts!

"Hey, man," Jackie then said to me, "we gotta go out on the road to support our hit. They want me at the Apollo, in Harlem, to open for the Marvellettes and the Exciters, and then to go on tour down to Florida! I'm going to need a road manager."

Believe me, I'd never felt so free in my life. This was a chance I had to jump at, because I *could.* "Man," I told Jackie, "I'd love to take that trip with you."

"Yeah, but can you?"

"Shit, yeah."

"All right then. Be my road manager."

Jackie offered four hundred dollars a week for the job, which sounded to me like a million. I accepted in a heartbeat. The only trouble was, I didn't know how to tell my wife and Mama I was going out for three months on this tour. I knew I had to get it all clear in my mind as well as theirs, because this was going to be the first time I'd ever left Los Angeles. It was important for me as well as them to know I'd be as close as the telephone, and should they need anything, I'd make sure they got it. Jackie gave me the first four hundred in advance, to take care of all my outstanding bills—especially the phone, so it wouldn't be cut off while I was gone.

Jackie and I set out by car from South Central, headed east. I was so excited I drove three days nonstop until I saw a sign that said New York City. The Lincoln Tunnel. We went under the river, came up on the other side, into that traffic that was so crazed, I'd never seen anything like it. I told Jackie to take over the wheel, because I couldn't handle it. He drove us to our hotel, after which we headed straight for the Apollo Theater. We were supposed to arrive on a Wednesday at twelve o'clock. We made it that day by 11:15. It was that close. Once more I thought about how destiny must have surely been riding shotgun for me these days.

It was during this gig I discovered I knew how to play pretty good sticks. It happened when I showed the drummer of the Apollo house band the roll-type rhythm on "The Duck." Jackie caught the moment, turned to me, and said, "Hey, I didn't know you could play the drums like that. Why don't you just do it yourself in the show?"

As with the piano, I had never had any formal training on the drums. I knew how to play them without ever actually having *played* them. When

I was a little boy I used to copy the drum sound from records, tapping out beats with my fingers on the edge of a table. As it turned out, I was so good that day at the Apollo that some of the other acts on the bill asked me to play drums for them as well, which allowed me to pick up an extra two hundred dollars a week. Although I was only originally there as a road manager, I suddenly found myself onstage, in the spotlight, playing in front of an audience, and they loved it!

They have a saying at the Apollo, that when you're a hit there a star is born. On the sixth day of our run, the management brought me the official house recognition for anyone who actually performed there—a folder with two pictures of me inside, one playing drums, another alone onstage, with the inscription A STAR IS BORN! What a moment!

I met a lot of new musicians the eight days we were on the bill, including the Exciters, Dee Sharp, and the Marvellettes. Bobby Rogers came to see his lady, Wanda, of the Marvellettes, and the legendary Smokey Robinson came with him. I got to meet both Bobby and Smokey, which for me was a tremendous thrill. They were smooth, they were dressed down, they were cold! Bobby asked what was happenin' and made it feel like he knew me! Right then and there I made myself a promise that if I ever became famous, I'd treat everybody the same warm way, no matter who they were, or weren't. I also met Johnny Isley, a cousin of the famed Isley Brothers. I was hanging out with the big boys now!

We did seven shows a day (two songs each act) and a matinee on Sunday. Every night, after the last performance, I'd go straight to bed.

One of the reasons I proved such a good road manager was because I never partied, I never went around with women, none of that. I took my paychecks, set out just enough money for me to eat, and always sent the rest home. Jackie may have been on a tour, but I was on a mission.

We left the Apollo Theater Sunday morning and headed out for Florida, with neither one of us having any idea how far from New York it actually was. In the meantime, because of our success at the Apollo we added some cities to the tour, and the route we drove took us, by necessity, straight through the heart of the Deep South.

In Hattiesburg, Mississippi, we got into a little trouble with some local rednecks at a restaurant. The police came by and, without even asking what happened, threw Jackie and me in jail for the night. One of the police said to me, "Boy, you don't know where you are . . ." He was so right.

We got released in the morning and blew out of there as fast as we could. We stopped next in Mobile, Alabama, and I decided to call Mary, to let her know I was all right. I went to a phone booth and said into the mouthpiece, "Baby, get me area code 213," and gave her my number.

"Just a minute, sir, the lines are tied up." I sat there waiting for her to come back on the line when the police showed up in their patrol cars, tires screeching. This time they were wearing cowboy hats with badges on them! One of them came over to me. "Hear you been using profanity on the phone, boy."

"What are you talking about?"

"Well," he said slowly, with a heavy Southern drawl, "you called our operator 'baby.' We don't do that down here. Where you from, boy?"

"California."

"See, that there's the reason you don't know. Our niggers, they know how to talk on the phone. They know you can't talk like that down here." That *really* pissed me off, but I held it in. The cat eventually did let me go, but not before giving me a warning that sent a chill up my back. "We get another call in this state that you called some operator 'baby,' you goin' to jail. Hear that, boy?"

Once again we got the hell out of town as fast as we could. We drove all day and that night, in Louisiana we decided to stay at one of those Travel Lodge–type hotels. As it happened, a couple of Klan members were also staying at the same place. I didn't sleep so well, thinking about those hooded dudes I'd seen when we checked in. The last thing I wanted was any more trouble, especially after our latest run-in with those Southern police boys. I was still tired when we got into the car the next morning. As I slowly started packing the trunk, I looked across the lot and saw eight of them coming out of two different rooms, all dressed up in their white sheets and hoods. I went back into our room and told Jackie.

"You're not going to believe this, but the Kluxers are right outside." Jackie Lee went crazy! You see, he was twenty years older and had grown up in the South. He knew how crazy these weirdos really were. Me, I'd never been east of South Central before and had no idea what this Klan thing was all about. He peeked out of the curtain to see if they'd left, saw they hadn't, and begged me to stay inside with him. I wasn't having any of it. I went back outside and continued to pack the car knowing that as I was doing so, one of them was staring long and hard at me.

So I looked right back at him. Believe me, if a white boy ever looked at me that way in L.A., his ass would have been gone. I don't know why, but thankfully, nothing happened. Maybe they had a lynching or something to go to and didn't want to be late. Whatever the reason, they left without incident. Still, dangerous air continued to hang heavy on this trip.

We finally got back on the road. I was driving and before I realized it, probably because of the rough night I'd had, I fell asleep at the wheel. According to witnesses, Jackie Lee and I went down a ravine, came out of it, went back down in it, and out *again,* without either of us getting so much as a scratch. It had to be destiny.

At our next stop, Jackie Lee checked with his home office, and they told him they'd added a date at some local high school prom. Trouble was, when we got there we realized it was for an all-white student body. We started the show and while Jackie Lee was singing, one of the kids shouted, "Hey, boy, you play the *fuckin'* 'Duck' for us, you hear?" Jackie Lee pretended he didn't hear and continued singing.

"HEY! GODDAMN IT, YOU PLAY 'THE DUCK.' "

Jackie Lee then told the crowd not to worry, that he was going to get to "The Duck."

"GODDAMN, DID YOU HEAR WHAT I SAID, YOU BLACK MOTHERFUCKER? PLAY 'THE DUCK.' "

At this point I stopped playing the drums, the band stopped playing, and Jackie Lee stopped singing. I could see that some violence was about to go down, starting with this one white boy. He seemed tough, all right, but I was tough as well. He couldn't approach Barry White or Jackie with his kind of attitude, because we had a street-gang mentality, one I was sure he'd never seen in his wildest dreams. I looked right at him down there in the audience and was about to tell him what I thought when Jackie Lee turned to me and said, *"Barry, let's play 'The Duck' for this motherfucker!"*

This *really* pissed the guy off!

Now, there was another act on the bill with us named Slim Harpo. Slim was a brother with a white girlfriend, and this was not the night to spread that news around. When we finished playing the gig, Slim decided that for safekeeping, he should put his girlfriend in the trunk of his car! I will never forget that. I soon learned he knew what he was doing, because when Jackie Lee and I headed for our car, there was a bunch of white boys from the audience *waiting* on us. I told Jackie Lee not to worry and went first. I had such a look on my face, like any *one* of you want to start some shit, *now's the time!*

They must have gotten the message, because all those boys did was whisper to each other as Jackie Lee and I walked right through them. He tried to get into the car quickly, but I told him not to speed up. Now wasn't the time to show fear, brother! We'd survived the redneck police, the Klan, and the car wreck, we could surely make it past a couple of schoolboys.

And we did. Even so, by now I was more than ready to leave the road behind for good. It had just been too difficult—too many warnings, too many close calls. I always pay attention to those kinds of warnings. I think most people get warnings before things happen and just aren't aware of them. But I'm not about to start moving at random in this cosmos. I suggested to Jackie Lee we forget about Florida, finish out the tour in New Orleans, and he agreed.

Mardi Gras! There we were in a club in the French Quarter. This was the first time I'd ever seen anything like this. It was wild time in the old town tonight! Everyone was drinking, dancing, stumbling, and dressed in crazy costumes. Out of nowhere, some local cat started talking to us, and the next thing I knew, a woman came up to him, called his name, and he fell over. She'd stuck him in the back with a knife and killed him!

That was absolutely the end for me. I'd had enough and went straight back to our motel room and locked myself in for the rest of the night. The next morning I woke up and told Jackie I was flying straight back to Los Angeles. I'd never been on a plane in my life, but I just couldn't wait to get off this tour. I called Delta Airlines and booked a flight. I'll never forget how shook up Jackie Lee was that I was going to fly home. He tried everything to get me to stay.

"Sorry, man, but I'm going."

At the last minute Jackie Lee left his car, his clothes, everything at the motel and went with me. He figured that once I saw my family I'd be all right and return to the road. He even offered me a raise, but I told him I wasn't going to leave Los Angeles *ever again.*

As it turned out, coming home early that March, instead of staying out through April as we'd originally planned, turned out to be a very good thing for me.

First, I managed to hook up with one of my childhood friends, Frank Wilson, the only kid from the 'hood I ever hung with who was as into music as I was. We first met in school when I was six and he was eight. He was coming down the steps and I was going up. We were both trying to act like little gang-bangers, and as we passed each other I hit him hard and knocked him down. Frank got up and kicked me down the steps. I was shocked. I got up, we looked at each other, shook hands, and began a friendship that, with a couple of unintended separations, has lasted fifty years.

Frank was now dating a girl named Charlotte, who happened to be the daughter of my next-door neighbors. The day after I got back home from the road he'd come by to see her. I was home, trying to work some-thing out on the piano. Frank heard it and knew my style so well he knocked on the door to find out if in fact it was me. Mary answered and when she told him it was indeed Barry White's place, he let out a long, low growl! As soon as I heard it I turned my head and shouted, "Frank Wilson!" I hadn't seen him in eight years, not since we each had to move to new neighborhoods.

He came in, we hugged, and did a lot of catching up. I found out that he was not only still into music, but the lead singer of the Remarkables, a local group with a hit record that had actually gone to number one in L.A.—"Is the Feeling Still There?" I'd loved the record when it came out, even though I had no idea at the time Frank was singing on it. So here we both were, still into music. We determined to stay in touch this time. Running into Frank meant a great deal to me. I felt that day as if I had made some spiritual reconnection to my musical roots.

The next morning brought me further proof that it had been a good thing to come home early. I received an unexpected phone call from one of the pickup session players I'd first met and worked with back in '62 by the name of Paul Politi.

"Barry," he said. "I'm glad I got you. Any chance you're looking for a job?"

"Depends. Doin' what?"

"Ever thought about becoming an A and R man? Bob Keane over at Mustang Bronco Records is looking for somebody and wants to talk to you about it. Can you be at his office tomorrow?"

"What's an A and R man?"

"I don't know. We'll figure it out after you get the job. Interested?"

I asked Paul if this was the same Bob Keane who worked with Sam Cooke and Richie Valens. Turned out it was, and he now had a happening group called the Bobby Fuller Four. As Paul and I talked, I started remem-bering some things I'd heard on the street about Bob Keane, and to be hon-est with you, it wasn't all that good. His previous label, Del-Fi Records, was notorious for having money troubles. Still, I figured there was no harm in meeting with him. I'd know soon enough if he was a wrong guy.

"Can you get there tomorrow morning?"

"What time?"

"Nine."

"I'll be there."

Bob Keane's office was in Hollywood, on Selma, one block over from where I made my first hundred dollars clapping out that rhythm. What a trip. It had taken me six years and thousands of miles to travel to the other side of the street.

I met with him in his office, and was feeling a bit nervous. Everything was happening so quickly, I hadn't even had time to get my clothes cleaned from the road. I must have put out a bad vibe, because after we talked, he told me rather coldly to wait outside while he met with Paul.

Keane told Paul he didn't think I had anything, and that's when Paul went to bat for me. "Please believe me, Bob, this guy is talented. He knows all these rhythm techniques, and he will work his ass off for you!"

Keane thought it over and agreed to give me a shot. He called me back into his office and right then and there offered to start me at a salary of forty dollars a week. Believe me, I appreciated the offer, but felt he wasn't convinced I was really worth it. So I said to him, "Mr. Keane, if forty dollars is too much money, you can pay me twenty and let me learn the ropes." My thinking was simple. It was a fifty-fifty trade-off. He wasn't going to get the benefit of my talent and abilities without my getting the benefit of his knowledge and experience. We shook hands and the next day I reported for work.

I took the bus every day to the office and was never late. I kept my eyes and ears open, and took in everything I could.

Four weeks later I was lucky enough to meet Hal Davis, one of the executives at Motown. The first thing I noticed about him was how great he was dressed. He told me he had all his clothes custom made at Cy Devore's of Hollywood. And then he offered me a bit of advice and did something I've never forgotten. He explained how in Hollywood everyone was always turning their wardrobe over, that it was the hip thing to do, and since he and I were both big boys, he gave me a complete set of clothes he no longer intended to wear. These were some of the coldest threads I'd ever seen. Beautiful shirts, slacks, jackets, everything I didn't have. The fact that another brother was looking out for me moved me so deeply. I started wearing my new clothes to the office every day. Somehow being able to dress the part helped me gain an enormous amount of confidence, and once again, things started happening in my favor.

So much so that six months later I was the vice president of the company.

I was now the executive in charge of Bob Keane's A&R division, the first steady job I'd ever had in the music business. A&R, which stands for "artist and repertoire," entails finding, developing, and producing artists and matching them with the right material to record.

Paul and I went through hundreds of acts, until I thought I'd finally found the right girl, who, with some work, might be good enough. Viola Wills was her name.

I called an old friend of mine from the church choir, a fellow by the name of Ronnie Gorrey, and asked him if he'd like to help me write some material for her. He agreed and we banged out a little tune called "Lost Without the Love of My Guide." Bob Keane looked at it and said I could make it for sixty dollars. In fact, he wanted me to make every record for sixty dollars. To save money, I wound up playing most of the instruments on these recordings myself.

Although the record didn't go anywhere, I felt triumphant. I had, for the first time, been able to find an artist, develop material for her, make a record, and get it into the marketplace. I'd accomplished something that as far as I'm concerned was worth as much to me as a gold record.

Bob then came to me and said, "I want you to find an act for me that sounds like Diana Ross." This turned out to be Felice Taylor. Bob quickly gave me the green light to sign her, and once again I had the chance to work from scratch with a new artist on a record.

Paul and I wrote a song for Felice called "It May Be Winter Outside (But in My Heart It's Spring)." We played it for Bob, who liked it but said there was something missing. We went back and made our lyrics even stronger. This time Bob really thought we nailed it, except for the hook.

He told me, "Barry, you can tell a great song from what you throw away. Get rid of that hook and put a different one in." I took that little nugget of wisdom and stored it in my memory bank, where it continues to gain interest for me to this day.

ONE DAY BOB told us his partner was coming by later in the week to look things over. Partner? I didn't even know he had one. I asked him who it was.

"His name is Larry Nunes and he's my major investor. In other words, the money man, kid. He is the guy who writes the checks."

Paul the janitor and I cleaned the entire office from floor to ceiling.

Larry Nunes, as it turned out, was more than just Bob Keane's money man. He was one of the key players in the early days of rock and roll. He developed the original independent rack-jobber method of out-of-the-trunk distribution and made a fortune out of it and a viable business out of what was then considered a passing fad, rock and roll. His success made him a real player, and he became close with some of the most colorful and controversial characters in music, including, among others, the infamous Morris Levy. Eventually, Nunes's distribution system was connected in one way or another to every independent and major record label in the country.

I'll never forget the first time I saw him, the night he arrived in person to check up on the company. He sported a spectacular outfit—black leather jacket, black shirt, black pants, black socks, black shoes. He looked for all the world to me like a *movie star,* complete with an entourage of six big bruisers behind him. He had a slight air of mystery about him, a regality to his Portuguese good looks. I loved his walk, I loved his talk. He had great style and personality. No question, Larry Nunes was *the man!*

Bob Keane introduced us, and I felt an instant chemistry. Larry Nunes shook my hand, smiled, and said warmly, "How you doin', *Barr?*" That's what he called me that first night and that's what he would call me the rest of his life. It was a term of endearment I came to love. I called him *"Larr"* in return, and these became our special, unique, and private names for each other.

Although I didn't know it, I'd already made a strong impression on Larry Nunes, and he was well aware of who I was in his organization. It turned out that when Bob Keane first played Viola's record for him, he liked it so much he personally took it to Big Jim Randolph, then the most powerful DJ at KGFJ, and that was how the record landed on the station's play list.

A few weeks later Larry Nunes took me aside and asked what I thought was wrong with the records we were making at Mustang, because no matter how hard he tried, he couldn't seem to break anything we gave him into a really big hit. I told him what I thought: Basically, Bob Keane was a great discoverer of talent, but producing wasn't his best skill. The next thing I knew, Bob asked me to take a shot at mixing our biggest act, Bobby Fuller. Until then Bob had done everything with Bobby by himself.

My experience with surfing bands now paid off. We cut an album in two weeks, after which Bobby paid me a great compliment when he told me that I was the most outrageous arranger he'd ever met. Once again my name started getting around. I was being talked about. *Bob Keane has this brother, Barry White, who knows how to make Top 40 hits for white kids.*

I then tried to move Frank Wilson and the Remarkables, who were damn good, to Bronco, but Keane just didn't hear it. Probably as a courtesy to me he offered Frank and his brother fifty dollars each a week as staff writers, which they took because they needed the money, but he had no faith in them, and they never went anywhere.

Around this time I hooked up again with Gene Page, my good friend from the old Bob and Earle days, when he too came to work for us. Gene managed to get us into a recording session at Motown's Hollywood studios. This was major for me, because it meant I would actually have the opportunity to watch my heroes, Holland, Dozier, and Holland, do their wondrous thing.

Eddie and Brian Holland, who were brothers, and their partner,

Lamont Dozier, had single-handedly shaped the sound of Motown, with numerous pop classics that included Marvin Gaye's "Can I Get a Witness?" and "How Sweet It Is (to Be Loved by You)"; Martha Reeves and the Vandellas' "Heatwave," "Quicksand," "Nowhere to Run," and "Jimmy Mack"; The Supremes' "Where Did Our Love Go," "Come See About Me," and "Stop! In the Name of Love"; the incredible string of Four Tops hits that included "Reach Out I'll Be There," "It's the Same Old Song," "Seven Rooms of Gloom," "Bernadette," and the absolutely phenomenal "Standing in the Shadows of Love." Eddie was the lyricist, Lamont supplied the melodies, and Brian produced the records. Their list of great songs goes on forever, and as far as I'm concerned, it's never been matched by *anyone* in the entire canon of rock and roll. They could write love songs in the form of romantic apology like no one else and if there's one thing they proved, it's that women love "I'm sorry" songs. These became H.D.H.'s grand theme and led their way to everlasting greatness.

They were who I wanted to be. What a great moment for me, breathing the same air as my lifelong idols.

At one point Brian Holland looked through the glass into the engineering booth where I was sitting and caught my eye, a purely spiritual experience. When the music started, I knew instantly that *that* was the sound still so elusive to the heart, ears, mind, and soul of not only Bob Keane but everyone I'd yet had the chance to work with in rock and roll. I could hear it in my head but had not yet found a way to really get it down on record. That day in the studio, I felt I'd taken a giant step closer to my goal.

FOR AS LONG as it lasted, Mustang Bronco proved a terrific learning experience for me. I never knew what to expect from one day to the next, like the time a kid named Jimmy Ford walked into our office with this shabby-looking country girl at his side. I could tell in a minute he was a strong songwriter, the real thing—gifted even—with a song that he, unfortunately, couldn't sing. There was too much of a Southern twang to his voice, which is why he wanted the girl to record it for him. I took the song, which I loved, to Bob and told him we had to buy it.

He listened to it, said it was awful, didn't think the girl had anything, and passed.

At the time Jimmy Ford was so desperate for money, just to pay his rent he was willing to sell the rights to the song outright for fifty dollars. I went back to Bob once more and tried to convince him, but it was no use. Five weeks later the song came out on Capitol, whose headquarters were right up the street from us, with that same shabby-looking little girl singing it. Her name was Bobbie Gentry and the song became the top-selling country crossover song of 1967: "Ode to Billy Joe."

The same thing happened again with another group at Mustang. They called themselves the Versatiles. They put down a lot of tracks for us, but only one that I really liked: "You're Good Enough for Me." It didn't really go anywhere, and they asked for their release. I liked them on a personal basis, and because I had the power to grant it, I gave them their freedom, along with their master tapes. As they were leaving I said to Mark Gordon, their manager, "The Versatiles are a great group, you just need to change their name." The next thing I knew they were calling themselves The Fifth Dimension, with hit after gigantic hit off those masters they originally recorded while at Mustang.

This kind of thing happened a lot there. Too often, if you ask me. On top of that, Bob Keane had to have what was the worst ongoing bad karma I've ever seen. Three of his biggest stars died, one after the other. Richie Valens, his first big act, was killed in that tragic 1959 plane crash, which also took the life of Buddy Holly. A few years later Sam Cooke, another of his artists, was shot to death by a disgruntled fan. In 1966 Bobby Fuller suffocated in his car.

Finally, in 1968, after a series of missed opportunities and songs that went nowhere, Larry Nunes decided to put his energies into his new company and shut the label down. The demise of Mustang Bronco broke my heart. I'd put everything I had into that daily grind, trying to make something work and then, suddenly, there was no more company.

I never wanted to be hurt like that again. The pain cut so deep I made a promise to myself that I would not work for another company as long as I lived.

One week after I left Mustang Bronco Records I ran into a charming, sophisticated little guy I knew named David Mook who happen to work for the hot new music kids in town, the publishing company of Aaron and Abby Schroeder. They'd already scored big in New York, having conquered Tin Pan Alley and the national Top 40 as the publisher of dozens of pop and rock acts. They were now out to do their thing in L.A. During the course of our conversation, David asked if I would meet with him at his office to talk about some songwriting gigs. He said they were interested in signing me on as a writer.

Now that really messed me up. My wounds were still fresh from Mustang Bronco—hell, I was still bleeding a little from Al Samuels, and now here was yet another dude who wanted me to go to work for someone. I guess the upside was that in spite of all my deep disappointments, I began to feel that I must somehow belong in this business, because these days whenever it looked like I'd hit a brick wall, there was always somebody who, based on my talent, wanted to take me around it and give me a job.

I desperately wanted to find a way to take one more chance on my music, and for that reason I agreed to meet the Schroeders.

However, before I even met with Aaron and Abby, I got another call from Motown, only this time it wasn't about sitting in on a session. It turned out they also knew who I was and were interested in hiring me based on a little song I'd written and recorded in 1966 while at Mustang with a guy by the name of Robert Staunton called "All in the Run of a Day."

Surely it seemed I had caught the ear of the boys at Motown, who were now interested in laying out a game plan they said would guarantee to make me a star. They thought I had a good voice, from the background vocals I'd done the past couple of years, and said they wanted to put me on their very impressive roster of writers, producers, *and artists*. They offered a heavy salary, expense account, use of a company credit card, all of it.

They told me everything I could possibly want to hear, and it made me very proud. I must have had every single record they'd ever released.

Still, in spite of everything, after listening to what they had to say, I politely but firmly turned them down. My close friend Frank Wilson thought I was out of my mind. He drove me to the meetings because I still didn't have a car, and after I told him what they were offering me and that I was going to turn it down, he said, "Barry, you have four kids and no money coming in. You should take that offer."

I explained to him that I just knew I didn't want to go that way. There was just too much of a chance of more big-time heartbreak there, and I'd had enough of that.

So instead, I paid what I thought would be that courtesy call on the Schroeders. They had offices in the 9000 building on Sunset Boulevard, one of the most famous and prestigious addresses in music. The high-rise was new, shiny, and black, and passing through its front doors felt magical to me, like a trip straight to the mainstream.

During our meeting, they told me they'd already signed Randy Newman, one of the most unique and gifted writers ever to come out of Sunset Boulevard's Music Row, and another newcomer by the name of Jimi Hendrix.

I liked that. The big thing for me was how they saw their company as one big family. I liked that as well. They then offered me four hundred dollars a week. It was tempting, and I surely needed the money, but in the end I still felt I had to say no. I explained to them how I just couldn't be anyone's hired gun again. Okay, they said, and asked me for an alternative plan. I thought about it and asked if I could be in business with them and for myself at the same time; if I could own my own publishing, in partnership with them. They said they were willing to take a chance on both my songs and me. That day we formed a company I named Savette Publishing. I knew I was going in the right direction when, before I'd written a single song for them, Aaron and Abby agreed to front me a small draw, enough to live on so I could write what they were sure were going to be big hits.

Over the years what began as a friendly business relationship developed into something extraordinary and unique. For the next thirty-one years, Abby did every bit of negotiation and contract work for me in my career, to make sure I was always well protected. She and Aaron are truly amazing people—honest and sincere—the rarest of breeds in the music business. They understand loyalty like few people I have ever met in any walk of life. Most publishers live by one sacred rule: Get the songs and ditch the writer. Aaron and Abby's way of doing business was, to me, radically different. They sought to protect the writer in the belief that doing so would help make better songs come from him. In 1974, when our contract ran out, Abby simply said that she and Aaron loved me, and that as long as I loved them back, we could continue to work together. If I stopped loving them for any reason I could simply close up shop and move on. "Think of us as a bow," she said. "As long as we're together, we're tight. When you want to leave, just let the string go and you're free." There are truly some things money can't buy, and loyalty, the kind that Aaron and Abby have shown me, and I have shown them, because it has to be a two-way street, is always going to be at the top of my list.

There were two more things I found out early on about Aaron that really blew me away. Ironically, I found them out *after* I decided to sign on with them. First, Aaron Schroeder, is, like me, a Virgo, and therefore a very powerful person. He began in the business as a songwriter and had written a considerable number of hits before deciding to go into publishing and producing, working with such big names as Gene Pitney; Blood, Sweat and Tears; Burt Bacharach and Hal David. That was kind of my story in reverse.

The second and truly amazing thing was that many of the biggest stars in the world recorded Aaron's songs, including Nat "King" Cole, Frank Sinatra, and . . . *Elvis Presley.*

Yes.

It sent a genuine icicle down my back the first time I found out *Aaron Schroeder had written Elvis's 1960 hit "It's Now or Never."* Aaron had sent out a time beam to me with that song, years before we were obviously destined to meet. When I found this out, I couldn't believe it! I was both stunned and thrilled, and sensed I had finally found my true cosmic and creative family.

FIVE

LOVE UNLIMITED

"WALKIN' IN THE RAIN WITH THE ONE I LOVE"

Oh, I'm just walkin' in the rain with the one I love
Feels so fine.
Walkin' in the rain with the one I love on my mind.
To each his own I've heard them say,
Well, I've got mine in so many ways.
Like being together,
Whether near or far
It doesn't matter where you are
So in love with each other
Giving love so warm and free made our dream a reality
Let it last forever and ever
With every step we take and every breath we make
Darling just you and me

THIS SONG TAKES PLACE in the rain. Woman meets man, woman loses man, woman meets a new man and moves on to a new life with renewed hope, optimism inspired by her revitalized feelings of love. Although this is a familiar formula for a love story that both men and women can and do identify with, I wanted to tell it here from the woman's point of view. Breakups are always hard, starting over difficult, the rebirth of love triumphant. The truth is that although we often think the end of a love means the end of everything meaningful in our lives, we can and do go on, we find new loves, and we try it all again.

The rain in the universe of my song represents teardrops, an expression of this woman's sadness we can all identify with, the cleansing or purification process, a ritualistic washing away of the tears of a love gone bad. The man who calls at the end is her savior. And that is my message, both in song and in life, that there is always someone to come along and dry your tears with the heat of a new fire in his heart and in his soul.

In song it might take a verse. In life it's not that fast or easy. The healing process from heartbreak can take awhile, but once you've pulled yourself together you mustn't dwell on the heartbreak. You have to know your own self-worth and get back into the game. Love really does heal. It is inside ourselves and waits for us to allow it to come out. If the key to our heart belongs to another, the heart itself still beats within . . .

"Walking in the Rain with the One I Love . . ." Yes, baby . . . yes . . . you understand that, don't you, baby? Walk with me now and I'll protect you and love you and keep you warm and dry and wrapped up tight inside my arms.

· · ·

IN JULY 1969 I met a girl named Andrea "Trixie" Robertson, who could plain sing her ass off as well as write. On my own, I scrambled around for some bucks to produce her. A small record company, Sidewalk Productions, headed by a guy named Danny Kessler, offered me a budget, and I wound up taking her into the studio and coming out with two terrific demos. What I didn't know at the time was that Sidewalk happened to be one of the many companies under the umbrella of Larry Nunes's new megacompany, Transcon. I hadn't seen or spoken to Larry since he'd closed Mustang. When Danny mentioned in passing that Larry was his money man is when I first discovered his Larry was also *my* Larry. *Karma!*

While in the studio with Andrea, she came up with the idea of adding some background singers she knew to the record. The three girls she wanted to use were all childhood friends, born and raised in San Pedro, where they'd gone to school, sang, and partied together. The next day, at Continental Studios on Hollywood Boulevard, I met the trio, all thin, pretty, black, well dressed, and still, for the most part, music wanna-bes with day jobs. Their names were Glodean James, a teacher's assistant, her sister, Linda James, a housewife, and their friend Diane "Dede" Parson, a factory worker. Then they sang "Are You Sure," a song they wrote themselves, and what can I say but that they knocked me out.

> *Are you sure that we're in love*
> *Are you sure our love is true*
> *Are you sure, are you sure, that we're in love . . .*

Andrea had been right on about these good-looking young ladies, they were very, very talented. Like every other black girl group in the 1960s, they had grown up with dreams of being the next Supremes. They called themselves the Croonettes and to this point had played mostly local gigs in the Long Beach area of Southern California.

One of them especially, Glodean, who sang lead, really caught my eye. She was playful, talented, and easy to get to know. She was soft-spoken yet had a very funny, sharp sense of humor and a wonderful way of saying what was on her mind that always put a smile on my face. Like Linda and Dede, she came off very innocent, which played into the sweetness of their performance, yet these honeys were nobody's fools. I talked to them for a while during one of our breaks, and they told me how a lot of hustlers had tried to run management games on them, but they'd been too smart to go for it. They knew they were pretty, and so did their parents, who'd warned them about the jungle Hollywood could be, filled with well-dressed wolves in sharkskin suits. It was one of the most refreshing conversations I'd had in a long time. I loved their manner, their awareness, and their open way of relating to me.

Maybe that's why it really didn't matter to me that they had no experience. I just loved the way they sang so much and thought their song had a fascinating, introspective quality about it. I knew right then and there that if they were willing to put the hard time and genuine effort into their singing and songwriting, they could produce incredible music. However, all they seemed to be interested in was singing backup for Andrea, and so, for the moment, that's where I left things.

After I finished all of Andrea's sessions, she said she wanted me to try to get her signed to ABC-Dunhill. I took the demos to ABC, where, not surprisingly, they immediately wanted to sign her. When I told Andrea, she was ecstatic, and then she dropped a little bomb. She really didn't want me to go along as her producer. She said she wanted to do everything she felt was creative herself (although perhaps she actually thought I might be an unnecessary expense when it came time to negotiate her deal). That was fine with me. I'll never stay where I'm not wanted, so I immediately cut her loose.

Three months later, her backup trio called me on their own and asked if we could get together for lunch. We made a date to meet at the Kabuki, on Crenshaw, a nice little Japanese restaurant that was, and still is, a favorite of mine.

While we were eating and small-talking, Linda suddenly looked up at me and said, in that cute manner of hers, "You don't love us, do you, Uncle Barry?"

They called me that from day one. Even though I was only twenty-four, because I was a big guy and the one in total charge of everything having to do with the making of my music, I appeared to them, and a lot of other people, to be older than I actually was. Older, but not old. That's why, instead of calling me something like "old man" or "Daddy," they chose "Uncle." I think it helped forge a special link between us as a term of great affection and endearment. I loved whenever they used it, but understand, they were the only ones who could call me that, the only ones I *allowed* to call me that. I also especially liked the fact that they only used it in private, when no one else was around.

"Of course I do, Linda. Why would you say something like that?"

"Because, Uncle Barry, you haven't asked to produce us."

She was right about that. I hadn't, because, as I said, as far as I was concerned they belonged to Andrea, and I didn't believe in poaching acts. However, now that they had come to me on their own, I felt that was no longer the situation. Linda said the girls wanted to make a single on their own and wanted me to produce it.

Their timing couldn't have been more perfect. They had that special sound I believed I knew exactly what to do with. There was something about the way they sang, undeveloped as it was, that spoke directly to me, the perfect embodiment for the kind of love songs I knew I was going to write. I'd been getting close, but I still hadn't found the right sound yet. I sensed I was about to make the leap to a place where I could create a more perfect world of love and romance with my music, a lush, perfect backdrop for the amorous adventures of all our lives. The problem was, I still hadn't found anyone who could inspire me with their voices; that is, until now.

Maybe, just maybe, these three young girls were the ones to lead me in the true direction of my artistic future. As soon as I started putting material together, I had a feeling I could write and produce not just one song, but a whole album around them. I decided to go for it!

When I told the girls, they became incredibly excited, and I knew I had to caution them about the realities of the music business. I warned them that almost no unknown artist ever gets a whole album produced and written by an unknown writer/producer. It was hard enough to get that financing for a single. I also told them not to expect a whole lot from a business that doesn't treat women, especially *black* women, all that well. I explained how I was willing to give them the benefit of my experience as well as my talent and that all I wanted in return was a real and total commitment from them. I'd see them through, I promised, if they stuck with it and me, and I'd get this album made. Not *try* to get it made, *would* get it made. I knew they were young, pretty girls with their whole lives ahead of them and that music wouldn't necessarily always be the most important thing. With that in mind, I also told them I expected them to see it through for at least five years, and after that, if they wanted to go their own ways, or leave the business entirely, hopefully there would be enough of a nest egg for them to be able to do anything they wanted.

They agreed, and we were off.

•   •   •

WE GOT TOGETHER and rehearsed every night for the next nine months. They kept their day jobs, while I tried to teach them everything I knew about the way I wanted to make records.

Early in 1970, they decided they wanted to leave everything behind they'd done till now, beginning with their name. "Uncle Barry," they said, "what should we call ourselves?" I told them I'd come up with something.

That night, at home, I was working with my friend and occasional cowriter Bobby Ralph, the other half of the old Bob and Earle duo, on a song we were calling "Love, We Finally Made It." After we finished and Bobby left, I sat in the dark, and suddenly it came to me. These were three such happy young girls, filled with good cheer and a willingness to go for it, so full of talent, beauty, and warmth, they were truly the living embodiment of *Love Unlimited*.

That was it! The perfect name for the perfect group. Immediately, the girls shot into my head. I could see their pretty faces, all sweet and smiling, laughing. They were dressed up in their sexy outfits, all the things about them that maybe weren't so obvious to anyone else that had blown my mind. There was no question, I saw them as an extension of my music, with no limits to where we could all take it. I rolled the words around in my mouth, to make sure they tasted as sweet, fresh, and tasty as my three girls. *Love Unlimited*. Delicious!

That is what I named them and that is precisely how I saw our relationship. The fabulous ladies of Love Unlimited. There were a lot of groups I could compare them to—the Three Degrees, the Emotions, the Supremes, all terrific, but none had that my-kind-of-wonderful onstage sound, presentation, style, and, yes, eroticism. Now, "wonderful" may not mean the same to everybody. To me, Love Unlimited was the very definition of wonderful—peaceful, sweet, innocent yet flirtatious, beautiful; they not only knew how to sing harmony, but they also were the living embodiment of it. They were so full of love every waking minute of the day.

The next night when the girls and I got together to rehearse, I gathered them all together and announced that from now on, they were Love Unlimited. They jumped up and down and squealed like the little innocents they were. They threw their arms around me and hugged and kissed me. "Uncle Barry! Uncle Barry! That's such a great name! Thank you, Uncle Barry!"

It seemed to make something click. We all got the feeling at the same time that something special was happening for all of us. From that night on, my songs began to ring from their mouths, their harmonies right in place, the sound we'd been searching for starting to emerge.

Enthusiastic as we were, it would be nearly another full year before I felt we had the material and the girls were good enough to look for someone to back the making of the album. During this time I was still in South Central, at home with Mary and the kids, and often visiting my mother, who had her own place close by. Although Mary and I were no longer living as husband and wife, we never wanted to put that burden on our parents, so we behaved civilly to each other and did the best we could to make our home environment appear warm and loving for our kids.

My mother was truly a godsend for Mary and me, always cooking and bringing over food for the kids, or taking them off our hands for extended visits with Grandma that helped relieve the tension and the pressure for me at home. I struggled hard to get the bills paid and worked with the girls every moment I had, squeezing in the writing of music whenever I had the chance. These were exciting, energizing, and difficult times, but also so stimulating, because I knew I was heading somewhere tangible, the big stop for the girls and me on that great glory train of music.

The girls were good students, but sometimes the going was slow. I had to give them, in effect, a complete music education from the University of Barry White. I had to show them where it came from, how the sounds were produced, what it meant to achieve a way of harmony that was unique, as well as how to move, how to look, how to *perform*. I was able to take them a long way, but you know how it is, the last flight of steps is usually the hardest, and as the months pushed on, I began to feel we were going to need something of a miracle to make that final leap.

Almost on cue, one came along when in August 1971, right after the girls had run through the material the best they'd ever done it, I got a call from Paul Politi.

"Barry," he said, "how are you doing?"

"Great," I told him, surprised to hear his voice. "I haven't seen you since the Bob Keane Mustang Bronco days, Doc."

We talked for a while and then he said, "Barry, I'm calling to tell you that Larry Nunes is looking for you."

LARR! "What does he want?"

"I think he's looking to start a production company with you."

"What?" I couldn't believe what I was hearing.

"Here's his number. Why don't you call him at his office right now?"

"I think I'll do just that." We hung up and I dialed the phone.

"This is Larry Nunes's office. Who's calling?"

"Barry White."

"Hold on, please."

"Larry Nunes's office. Who's calling?"

"Barry White."

"Hold on, please."

"Larry Nunes's office. Who's calling?"

"Barry White."

Three secretaries! I knew this guy was bad, but not *this* bad.

Finally he came to the phone, and I heard that familiar roar! *"Barr!"*

Hearing his voice felt as good as hearing my mother's. "Hey, Larry . . ."

"How you been, man?"

"Okay, but strugglin' like a son of a bitch."

"I hear you."

"Paul Politi told me to call you. What do you need, man?" I didn't want to say what Paul said, I wanted to hear it for myself.

"Barr, I want to go into business with you."

"Hey, you know, I'm down on my knees, man, I haven't got a dime to contribute."

"I'm not talking about money. I want to go into *production* with you. Can you get up to my office so we can talk about it?"

He was in Compton, as it happened, just up the street from Dede's house, where the girls and I had been rehearsing every night. "Surely I can."

I arrived about an hour later, and spent the rest of the day waiting to see him, before going home at five o'clock having gotten no farther than the waiting room. Then, just as I was about to leave, Larry's voice came ripping through the intercom. *"Barr,"* he shouted, "I'm sorry I couldn't make it today. Can you come back tomorrow?"

I told him fine, no problem, I'd be there.

Right on time the next day I returned and this time one of his assistants immediately escorted me into Larry's private office. He greeted me with a huge grin and a bear hug, and apologized again for having been tied up the day before.

I couldn't get over the cat. The last time I saw him, which had to have been at least four years, he was dressed all in black, and here he was again, still dressed all in black, with the same mannerisms, the same style. *Consistent.*

We talked for a while, during which time he filled me in on how he'd sold or merged all his various companies into one conglomerate called Transcon, which in turn had hired him to run it. Then he asked me what I was working on.

"Larr, I have three of the most beautiful and talented girls you've ever seen in your life."

"Great. What are you calling them?"

"Love Unlimited."

He sat back down in his chair, smiled, and said softly, "I love that name."

"These three women are sacred to me, man. They put a voice on the music I hear in my head."

"That's great. So what's the problem?"

"The same everyone else has, Larry. I don't have the money to get us off the ground."

"Well, you go home tonight and figure out how much you need to cut your album, and call me in the morning."

I couldn't believe this! *Figure out how much I need?*

"Hey, you want a drink, Barry?" I rarely ever drank anymore, but this time I said yes. Sure enough, after we each had a shot, he hit me with the big one.

"Well," he said, "I want you to become partners in an operation I'm going to call 'Mo' Soul Productions.' I'll give you twenty-four percent of it, the rest to be divided among my sons. You run it, record your group, and keep the publishing on all your songs. How does that sound to you?"

I couldn't believe it. Here I was, without a dime to my name, with a group I couldn't afford to record, with nothing but *my knowledge of music.* And over there was Larry Nunes, a millionaire, offering me not just a way to make a decent living, but the opportunity to make *my musical life!* The first thing I said was, "Hey, man, you don't have to give me anything, I'll work hard for my end. You see, it's not about your money, it's about my self-worth."

"Don't worry," he said with a chuckle. "You'll work hard for your percentage. Now you put that budget together for Love Unlimited, and let me hear them when you think they're ready."

I stayed up all night. When I returned the next day I had the numbers all worked out. He greeted me with the usual shout and bear hug and then I showed him what I had. I gritted my teeth, hoping he didn't say it was too much. "Thirty-two thousand five hundred dollars," I said, to break the silence. "That's how much I need to make this album."

I looked everywhere in that room except at him, because I couldn't bear to see what I feared would be the face of rejection staring back at me.

"This looks fine, Barry," he said finally. "And you're ready to go?"

"I could be, Larr, but with three more months' rehearsal I could get it exactly right."

"No problem. I'll give you the money now, in cash. You take the time and go the way you want. You'll also need some money to live on, to support your family, and the girls, they'll need a few bucks too." He asked me for their names, and then reached for the phone to tell his assistant to have a thousand-dollar check drawn up for each of them. "And, oh yes, make Barry's for three."

It was one of the hardest things I'd ever had to do, but I told him to hold on to his money until we were ready. He smiled, put the phone down, and told me how much he loved and appreciated my honesty, how rare it was in the business we were in.

The business we were in. I liked that!

WE REHEARSED EVERY night nonstop for the next three months, during which time I discovered how difficult it was to make the leap from very good to great. There were times I felt it was never going to happen, that getting the music from my head to their throats was about as difficult as climbing Mount Everest. The big problem was that all three girls were painfully shy, which affected their ability to take the extra step to where I needed them to go. I knew I had to help them build up their self-confidence to get them to perform at their best.

I loved the energy and enthusiasm they brought to the studio, but they always seemed to leave it in the other room when it came time to show themselves off. They were young, they were nervous, and they were inexperienced.

My disappointment and frustration finally expressed itself as anger. One night I told the girls to come back when they wanted to get serious, and sent them home. I didn't call them again for five days. When I finally did, Glodean took the phone and burst out crying, saying they didn't know what happened but could they "please have one more chance, Uncle Barry?"

From that day on, I worked them so hard I went, in their eyes, from the kindly Uncle Barry to the mean, tyrannical one. Except for Glodean. Because, in the past few weeks, in the middle of all this hard work, we'd started *liking* each other. I remember exactly how it began. I was over her house poring over her record collection and was surprised when I found a copy of "It May Be Winter Outside (But in my Heart It's Spring)," the record for Felice Taylor I'd worked on at Mustang Bronco. When I told Glodean I'd produced it, she didn't believe me at first, until I showed her the small-print B. WHITE under the title. She was impressed, to say the least.

Then, one night not long after, while I was at her place again, out of nowhere she asked me if I could dance. *Could I dance?* I told her how, when I was a kid, I'd been the baddest dancer in the 'hood. I smiled, asked her to put a record on, and showed her some of my moves. I was a bit bigger than I'd been as a teenager, but I could still move it, I could still do my *thang!* Baby, I was hot!

The next thing I knew we were kissing, liking it, and wanting to do it again. After that day we wanted to be alone together whenever we could. She wanted to know everything about me, especially how I wrote the songs I did, where they came from. I told her all about the stories I saw in my head and how I was inspired through music to shape my perfect world, a world that now included her in such a beautiful, intimate way.

I knew now I could no longer live under the same roof with Mary. One night I packed my bags and decided the time had come to move out.

Larry Nunes lived in a gorgeous house in Sherman Oaks, a part of North Hollywood known as the Valley that overlooked the 101 Freeway and seemed to me about as exotic and remote from South Central as anyone could get. I often stayed overnight in his guest house. Now I knew I needed my own place. In 1971, I moved into the Franklin Arms Hotel, in West Hollywood, one block north of Hollywood Boulevard—a place which I happily shared with Glodean.

And that is where, one night, we made love for the very first time. It was one of the most amazing moments of my life. I had that feeling one gets very rarely in life, when the creative spark ignites the flames of love and your house of passion goes up in one glorious blast of hot flames. I was with the woman I loved, writing music she had inspired, music that in turn brought us closer together and deeper in love, and I couldn't get enough. I never wanted that night, that feeling to end. I felt engulfed and liberated all at once. I was in love, and love became the grand theme of my life, my work, my soul, and my bliss. Right then and there, at that precise moment, I knew I had made it; I had become successful in the most profoundly meaningful way possible.

We made love deep into the night, and for the both of us it felt like the first time we'd ever been in another's arms. Maybe in some ways that was true, that this was our "first time" in this new terrain of true love. For me, it felt like an eternity since I'd been with a woman. My marriage to Mary had ended so early and so badly, I'd been turned off to the idea of the union of passion and women. Now I had been rescued, resurrected, rejuvenated, and born into a world of privilege, a free and open world where love and beauty and feelings and joy were truly boundless.

My feelings for Glodean were so different from anything I'd known before. This was no ghetto romance, born of frustration and false hopes. This was a love that was also a union, a creative union in which I had found the physical embodiment of all that was sweet and caring and *feminine* within my artistic body and soul.

One night in 1974, after we'd been together awhile, shaken up our worlds and joined our hearts, I got up while she slept and went into the kitchen and started writing the song that would become one of my signatures, "Can't Get Enough of Your Love, Babe," my musical tribute to Glodean. Although in time everyone would know this song, these words, for now I wanted it to be only for Glodean. It was a private love letter with rhyme and melody, something to keep between us until I was ready, until I knew how to properly and respectfully present our private love song to the whole world. This was one the girls weren't going to be able to sing, and one I wanted no one else to be a part of.

My darlin',
I can't get enough of your love, babe,

Girl, I don't know, I don't know why,
Can't get enough of your love, babe

What had begun as a working friendship had become a passionate love affair, fueled by a creative and emotional bond that would last between us, in one form or another, the rest of our lives. I had written this song for her as my way of reaffirming my innermost feelings. I was in an extended state of ecstasy, a result of our physical and emotional union. Here was a woman I could relate to on every level, a woman who not only understood me as a musician but *loved* me for it. Here was a woman who came as close as anyone to personifying my Lady Music. I wanted to give her something that night that came from the deepest and most sincere part of me.

OF COURSE, from the very beginning of my days with Love Unlimited, I never let my feelings for Glodean interfere with the special dynamic of

the group. In many ways, it actually enhanced it. We eventually became like one big crazy family, as if Glodean and I had these two terrific daughters, even though the girls were all within a year or two of each other. We understood it without having to verbally define it and took great joy from our tightness. Linda and Dede knew that even though Glodean and I were a couple, I loved them all as close and dear as any friends I'd ever had, and I knew that they loved me.

We worked harder than ever now to get our material together. We were on a mission together, and we would succeed or fail as one.

When I finally felt they were ready we went back into the studio, and this time the girls nailed it to the floor! They had conquered their fears and put the music over. I mean, they sang their hearts out! Afterward I gave them all big kisses and hugs. The magic we made that day would follow us right on to the stage and help make our live shows such special events, not only for the audience but for us as well.

I called Larry Nunes and told him we were ready.

"All right," Larry said. "Come by the office tomorrow, and bring the girls."

We arrived at one-thirty, and Larry himself came out to the reception area. He took us into his private office and handed me an envelope filled with cash. "All I'm going to ask you to guarantee is that you will give it your best shot. Make it happen, Barry."

Make it happen, Barry. That *did* it all for me. Here was a man who was putting not just his faith in me but his money where his faith was. No one had ever done that for me before. Just as we were about to leave, he said to me softly, "After this day you will want for nothing."

I believed him, because I believed *in* him, as much as he believed in the girls and me.

IN OCTOBER 1971, I set my sights on finishing the album by Thanksgiving Eve. That gave me about seven weeks to put everything I'd learned in my musical life, from my days as a little boy listening to those 45s alone in my room, into play. Every album, every record, every melody I had ever heard helped serve as the springboard for the making of this album. I knew it was my first big chance, but it also could have been my last. It was my moment of creative truth. *It was now or never!*

Because Larry Nunes had infused my spirit and inspired it with his faith, I made myself a promise that I would not let this man or myself down. In truth, there was very little distinction between us in our dedication. He was, in a very real sense, my show-business godfather.

It was just at this time my real father got the opportunity to meet Larry. I brought my dad to the studio one day, and as it happened, this was the only day Larry showed up during the entire recording process. I introduced them to each other and during a break in the session Larry told my dad, "You're very fortunate to be the father of Barry White." That is something he or I would never forget. Not that long ago my father had tried to convince me to give up music and get a "real" job. If I'd wanted to, for a million different reasons, starting with his not being around when my mother, Darryl, and I needed him, I could have built a pretty good case for cutting him out of my life. However, I wasn't about to do that. I had a lot of compassion for my father. He was a decent man and had tried to live life the best way he could. He was a complicated man, trapped in an economic and social world that severely limited his opportunities and I believe never truly happy in anything he did or with anyone he loved. He was, before and after everything in my life, my father, the man from whose seed I had sprung. He had given me life, and if he was big enough to come to me and tell me how proud he was, then I wasn't going to be too big to put my arms around him and give him the hugs and kisses he deserved. I wanted to love my father, not hate him. I wanted him to be proud of me, not envious. I wanted him to know that to me, family was everything, and he was as much a part of my family as anyone else. He was a man, and now I was one too and I understood that rough, tumbling, hard edge that was his exterior protection against the world. To turn him out would be to show proof that I had inherited the wrong legacy from his soul. I needed him to know that I was bigger than that and would be there for him for the rest of his life. I loved him in my way and he loved me in his. Although it had taken some time, we had found a place, no matter how awkward, to tell each other that. There's an expression that goes "The son is the father to the man." This was my chance to show what I was made of, to demonstrate my compassion and my humanity, and I wasn't going to blow it.

A few years later, as he was entering the hospital to be treated for cancer, my dad called me on the phone and repeated those very same words to me. "I am very fortunate to be the father of Barry White." They became the last he said to me before he died. I took it as some kind of strange and beautiful affirmation of the special link between father, son, and spiritual advisor that forever mingled our three souls.

THERE WAS ONE SONG I was still working on for the album that kept on giving me trouble. I'd come up with a couple of melodies and some chord changes that went together well, but for a solid year I couldn't find the lyrics to go with them. Then, one night, while sleeping, they came to me, complete, in a dream. I saw the words clearly in front of me. I woke up and immediately wrote them down. I was half asleep but kept writing, feverishly, so as not to lose any of them. Earlier that day it had rained particularly hard, and during the session I'd decided to record it. I'd always loved the sound of rain, and stuck a little Sony microphone out the window to see if I could capture it. The song I finished that night was "Walking in the Rain with the One I Love."

It proved the key. It gave me a theme, a completed cycle of related songs about old and renewed love, as seen from a woman's point of view. I decided to call the album *From a Girl's Point of View, We Give to You Love Unlimited.*

I saved "Walkin' in the Rain" for the last cut. It was a song whose theme gave the album its weight: one of the classic, romance-inspired and inspiring themes—two people meet, go together, break up, and then move on to new loves. On the last cut, after breaking up with her boyfriend for good, the girl walks home in the rain and gets a call from her new man. I was going to play that part myself.

After we finished recording the basic track, I sent everyone, including the girls, home for the night. I was about to do my telephone part when I noticed, looking out the window, it had started to rain. I decided to record it and stuck the microphone out the window.

I also did my audio track right then and there. My engineer fixed the phone so that when I picked it up, it went directly into the twenty-four track. There was nobody on the other end. I said, "Hello," and then pictured in my mind Glodean saying her part. "I'm home." Then I added, "Did you get caught in the rain?" I knew what her lyric was going to be. *"Oh, yes, it was so beautiful."*

The next day I had her rerecord her part, only this time to the track that I had recorded the night before. She couldn't believe what I had done! It became the opening of the last cut of the album.

That was it. With "Walkin' in the Rain" finished, I knew the album was done as well.

The night before Thanksgiving, I took the master dub to Larry's house and played it for him. He said nothing, and then, when it was finished, started crying. With tears in his eyes he turned to me and said simply, "Nice job, Barry. Well done."

I'll never forget that moment as long as I live.

SIX

WHITE HEAT

"I'M GONNA LOVE YOU JUST A LITTLE MORE, BABY"

Give it up, ain't no use
I can't help myself if I wanted to,
I'm hung up, no doubt,
I'm so in love with you,
For me there's no way out,
'Cause . . . deeper and deeper in love with you I'm falling,
Sweeter and sweeter the tender world of love you call it,
Eager and eager, yeah, to feel your lips upon my face,
Please her and please her anytime or any place.
I'm gonna love you, love you, love you
Just a little more, babe,
I'm gonna need you, need you, need you everyday, yeah,
I'm gonna want you, want you, want you in ev'ry way, yeah
Out o' sight . . . far out . . .
Hold back, no way
This time it looks like love is here to stay,
As long as I shall live,
I'll give you all I have and all I have to give.

E VERY WOMAN *and every man feels and hears their own thing when they listen to music. Women have a special insight on certain things that most men cannot comprehend. They react sensitively when they hear the sound of a chord change or the flow of a lyric. Women can pull things from that. They are attracted to pretty things, be it colorful flowers or a beautiful song, and feel them in a special way. It is a truly wondrous power. Men, on the other hand, identify with the delivery of that message. They hear themselves amplified through my voice and my words, set to the sounds of music, music that makes them want to get close to their woman. My recordings have always been majestic and intimate, powerful yet gentle, loving and alluring. My sound appeals viscerally to both men and women. There is a warmth beyond heat, an embrace that encloses within the arms of love. When women and men hear it, either separately or together, they know exactly what it means to each of them. My voice, my songs, my presentation are road maps they take with them as guidelines along the path of love. The world of my music is very romantic and ideal. The world everyone wants to live in. The world I wished we all shared. A song is just a song, unless it awakens someone to a way of life that hasn't been experienced before. Love is just love unless you do something with it. "Love" doesn't "love" anybody or anything. The idealism in my music is meant to show you what I've learned, and I hope, by example, it will teach you something about how to live your own life to its romantic fullest.*

My songs deliver the words that lovers may not speak aloud but want to hear themselves say or have said to them. My mood is always romantic, my words always upbeat, my message always the same: If you love someone you must not be afraid to tell them, to show them, to lead them to your heart. Lovers, hear me, follow this path I lay out before you. My music is the sound-track of your courtship, the gentle urging to take a hand, to brush against a lip, to put a head on a shoulder, to stroke a chin. My serenades celebrate the union between two people, one long nod of approval. I'm with you every step of the way, that's why I sing for you, that's why you play me, that's why you know your heart will lead you better than your head. . . . Remember, life is a love song that comes all in the run of a day. Be free to let yourself be enraptured by its music.

· · ·

LARRY NUNES TOOK the master dub of the Love Unlimited album to Russ Regan, the head of A&R for UNI Records, then the happening music division of MCA. Russ had a strong reputation for discovering talent. Whether Russ Regan was a canny executive with a terrific ear or extremely lucky with a tin one, by 1972 he was one of the new L.A.-based corporate superstars. Among acts he'd previously turned into major stars were Elton John, Olivia Newton-John, and Neil Diamond. Regan arranged to hear the album first before Larry could even play it for anyone else, loved it, and signed us to UNI.

The girls and I were ecstatic. I had promised I would see them through to a deal, and now, Larry Nunes, a man I considered nothing less than my savior, had helped make it come true.

"Walkin' " was the first single, behind which we hit the road for a long cross-country tour.

This was to be our first time out of Los Angeles, and I wanted to show the girls, and especially Glodean, the big world that awaited us now with open arms. I also wanted to protect them, to make sure they didn't have the kind of experience I'd had with Jackie Lee. I wanted them to benefit from my experience and to see only the good side of the country that now had their song on the radio somewhere every minute, every hour, every day of every week.

Sure enough, it hit the charts running, and we were sitting on top of the beautiful world we had idealized in our music. We were stars now and were ready to meet our fans! The excitement in the air was unbelievable. Every moment we were awake seemed like something out of a giant Technicolor movie. The road to Oz, that was the glory road we were about to dance on as we made our way across this great land.

When we went out on the road I was totally in charge, as I had been in the studio. I looked out for their welfare and kept all the sharks at bay. I also served as the girls' writer, producer, arranger, and musical conductor. We took along five horns, two guitars, a drummer, and a bass player, and I played keyboards.

I wanted the girls to look great as well as sound great. Because they were such an incredibly classy act, I wanted them to play the part from the tips of their polished fingernails to the sequins on their sparkling outfits. The clothes they wore, which they picked out themselves and later designed, were gorgeous, although I must tell you shopping with them was a nightmare. One time we spent an entire day looking for shoes, and unless you've been with three young ladies ripping through every pair in Hollywood, brother, you haven't lived. We went to eleven stores, and finally wound up back at the first one, where we'd started. It was the same kind of obsessive attention to detail they brought with them to the stage. From the moment the spotlight hit, they were *on it,* the most beautiful and stylishly entertaining female act anyone had ever seen.

I used to look in their eyes just before they went on and every night I could still see the familiar nervousness. I had worked with them relentlessly to find a way to channel that energy into an even higher level of onstage greatness. That's when I realized our two years of intense rehearsing really paid off. I took great pride knowing I had turned these girls into slick, professional, high-caliber performers. Audiences simply loved the drama and the romance of the show, highlighted by the rich erotic power of what was always our climax, "Walkin' in the Rain." That song became a performance piece all by itself, and always drove the girls and boys wild in their seats. It became everybody's living embodiment of romantic fantasy, lush with fabulous string arrangements. They always opened with "Oh

Love, We Finally Made It,"
my oh my you don't know how
long I've waited. . . . Every time
they'd begin to sing, I'd smile
and think to myself, yes we
did, ladies, yes we did!

They hit every note, made
every gesture, moved every way
they had been taught by me
to best tell our story through
song. Indeed, this was more
than just a show for us. It was
the ultimate culmination of
everything we'd hoped to become, and had. It also gave us
the opportunity to show the
world how much we meant to each other.

We were *cold!*

Onstage, Dede was the spokesperson because she had perfect diction.
Linda, however, was the magnet for the men in the audience. They used
to gravitate toward her during the show and call her name out loud. I used
to explain to the girls between shows that the audience loved Nanie, as we
all called Linda, so much because she was a Capricorn and therefore carried the spirit of Love Unlimited within her.

We had a lot of fun on the road, ordering everything on the room service menus and sampling each dish, having pillow fights in the halls of hotels, and playing jokes on each other just like we were one big happy family of brothers and sisters. Linda and Dede had boyfriends back home,
and they never worried about a thing, *never,* because they knew I was
watching over their ladies for them. Protecting them was all a part of what
I considered my duties. They were, after all, my songbird babies!

We were so tight by the end of the tour that when we came off the
road I told the other two girls I didn't want to see them again for a good
two months and was sure they didn't want to see me. We all agreed, but

just two days later we got back together and continued having the greatest time. By now I loved them to the deepest core of my being and would have willingly laid down my life for them.

The single went on to sell a million copies, and, in 1972, we had our first gold record. We couldn't believe it! We were on top of the world, man! The latest show business "overnight" success, right? Of course, no one wanted to hear about the eleven years it had taken me to find those couple of minutes of music that made the world embrace me like a mother and her newest-born baby. Show business is such a funny old world.

Perhaps the sweetest and most private moment of all during this time for me was when I gave my father a copy of the single. He listened to it through and said, "You know, Barry, this ain't my kind of music, I'm really much more into hard R and B, but I'll tell you, son, I really like this song." That, too, was gold to me.

So I had finally made it! From the nowhere of anonymity, I had taken a dizzying ride with my girls and together we had risen to the top of the charts. Here I was, sharing Top-10 space with my *idols,* Holland,

Dozier and Holland, and Marvin Gaye. I remember one day not long after the tour ended, I'd decided to take a walk down Hollywood Boulevard, and all I could hear from the record store windows were H.D.H. Motown songs, Marvin's fantastic "What's Goin' On" and "Walkin' in the Rain." I had never previously known any single greater feeling.

· · ·

LOVE UNLIMITED HAD succeeded in expressing my "female" side. Now I was intent on finding a male artist who could properly express the other, male side of my musical romantic equation. However, when I told Russ what I wanted to do, he didn't immediately go for it. Instead, he insisted I work on the obvious: a follow-up Love Unlimited album. He kept asking me why I wanted to fool with success.

Undaunted, I sat down one night shortly after the tour ended and in a burst wrote three completely new songs: "I'm Gonna Love You Just a Little More, Baby," "I Found Someone," and "I've Got So Much to Give."

Where did these new songs come from? I'll let you in on a little secret. Although they have always been considered among my most romantic pieces, the truth is, there are several levels of meaning to them, and they operate for me on all of them, within a unified theme. On one level, they are my great love songs, my testaments of intensity to Glodean. On another, they're really all about Larry Nunes—*"I found someone, I've got so much to give, and do all the things that I've longed to do . . ."* And on still another, they are about the years I spent preparing to make this creative leap into my world of musical artistry.

It was one thing to write songs for someone as a job and quite another to be able to reach deep inside the essence of my creative soul to find the words to express my feelings. To have Glodean share these glorious moments of my creativity, in the private solitude of our love and in the grandeur of the concert stage, made it all that much greater. To lead her and the others in every way made me feel like I was the luckiest and happiest man in the world. My baby loved my music and always let me know how good it made her feel to know she was my woman. I loved being in love with a woman with such a wonderful sense of who I was; at my side, on stage, in bed, connected to my heart. She was the first person I saw when I opened my eyes every day and the last when I closed them at night. These were truly joyous days.

Once I had these songs, I laid down some demos, using myself on the vocals. One afternoon, a few days later, as I was sitting at the board listening to the playback, it suddenly hit me—*BOOOM!* My stomach flip-flopped so bad it scared me when I suddenly realized there was only one artist I knew of who could sing these love songs the way I wrote them, and his name was *Barry White!*

You may think this made me happy and that I thought I had solved all my problems, and you'd be wrong. You see, I knew I had a good voice long before that day. The truth was, my entire adult life people had been telling me how great my voice was. You know, I could be in a hallway talking to someone and a stranger would come out of the blue and say, "What a beautiful sound you have to your voice, young man. Do you sing?" It never meant anything to me, even when I did backup on other people's records to make some quick money or to help out a friend. I never allowed anyone to put my name on their records as one of the voices.

I just didn't want to be known as a singer. The way I saw it, in those days at least, singers carried a stigma: They were either "stupid," or "leeches," or "crybabies." No one in the industry respected them as artists. No matter who it was, or how much the public adored them, off the stage or out of the studio performers were considered the bottom of the barrel, and I didn't want any part of it. I really always and only wanted to be an A&R man, to play to my strength in the studio and behind the scenes. I wanted to develop and guide other artists, like Love Unlimited, rather than be one myself.

It wasn't until I had my producing ears on that I finally "heard" the voice of Barry White. For the first time, I became fully aware of the uniqueness, the powerful romantic pull, the emotional depth of the lure of my own voice. That's when I realized *I* was the artist I should be recording.

However, although I could hear for myself the magic that was clearly there, I didn't think I had the stomach or temperament to pull it off. The thought of actually standing in front of a microphone and singing my own music scared me a little. So, for the next several weeks, whenever anyone asked if I've found my male singer yet, I'd stall. When Larry Nunes asked, for the one and only time in my life, I lied to him and said that I had heard a new artist who might be good enough. When he asked me his name, I told him I was going to call him "White Heat."

This went on until I couldn't stand it any longer and had to tell Larry the truth—that "White Heat" was really Barry White. "Larry," I said, "I have found someone with a sound that is very unique, and that someone is . . . *me*. The only thing is, I don't want to be a singer. What am I going to do?"

We debated this the entire weekend. "If you really love me, you'll do it for me," he said.

"But, Larry, I don't want to sing."

"If you love me, you'll do it for me!"

What could I say? I owed the man my entire career. "All right," I finally said, somewhat reluctantly. "If that's what you want, I'll sing these songs myself."

Behind Larry's confidence and money, I went into the studio, and those songs came out of me like firepower from a cannon. I was on a tear. I quickly wrote two more and rearranged another Holland-Dozier-Holland favorite—the Four Tops' great hit "Standing in the Shadows of Love." Having done that, I felt the album was finished.

Russ Regan, meanwhile, had, at least partly because of the success of Love Unlimited, moved up from UNI to Twentieth Century Records. When Larry and I told him we were going back into the studio, he eagerly put up the money to make the new album.

What can I say, when it was finished, Russ hated it! As soon as he heard it, with a full orchestra behind it, with only five long, radio-unfriendly songs, he decided to pass. I couldn't believe this! As a personal favor to me, I asked him to call in José Wilson, the head of promotion for black artists at Twentieth Century, for a second opinion. José agreed the album had little commercial potential.

Russ gave Larry permission to shop the album.

I couldn't believe what I was hearing. I looked at Russ, then turned to Larry and said simply, "Let's go."

Larry saw the hurt in my eyes and patted me softly on the back. "Don't worry about it" was all he said. "We'll have a deal somewhere before this day is through."

What happened next was like something out of one of those old Keystone Kops comedies I used to watch Saturday mornings on TV when I was a kid. Larry and I got into his Eldorado and rushed around town trying to make a fast deal with another label. To Larry, this was like the old days, when he had a trunk filled with records he needed to unload. He was fast, he was smart, and he was convincing. The only thing he wasn't most of that day was successful.

The first place we went to was A&M. Chuck Kaye, the big A&R gun there, gave it an immediate listen to and said he didn't hear it. We thanked him and went up the street to Russ Regan's former label, UNI. Larry took the demo right in to Joe Sutton, the president of the company. He didn't hear it either. I couldn't believe I had been that far off! My whole life, I knew a hit record when I heard it. What, I wondered, was the matter with these guys?

We got back into Larry's car and he said, "Let's take one more shot with a friend of mine at CBS, Jack Gold. If he doesn't like it, then we'll have to rethink everything." Jack let us play it for him, and, what can I say except that he flipped out for it after hearing only two cuts!

"I want to call Clive right now," Jack said excitedly. He direct-dialed Clive Davis in New York and over the phone played him the first half of "Standing in the Shadows of Love." I could hear Clive screaming over the speakerphone. "I want that artist! I'll be out on the coast on Sunday to sign him."

We had done it! After this crazy, seesaw, wild and wonderful day that had seen me flirt with hitting bottom, I had landed on my feet, back on top of my world!

T R U E   T O   H I S   W O R D , that Sunday Clive came out to the coast. By the end of the next week we had worked a deal that gave us a seventy-five-thousand-dollar advance against royalties for the album. As it only cost thirty thousand to produce, this naturally made Larry and me very happy. We could pay off Russ's entire investment and still have quite a bit left over. That night we partied and as I often did, I stayed over in the guest room at Larry's house in Sherman Oaks. By the time I went to sleep I was exhilarated and exhausted.

The next morning was a Saturday. Larry's phone began ringing at twenty minutes after six. Its loud sound woke me up. A few minutes later Larry buzzed me on the intercom.

"Barry, pick up the phone." His voice was steady and he didn't say who it was. Because of the hour, I feared the worst, like maybe something had happened to one of my kids.

"Hello?"

"Barry?"

Russ Regan. What a relief! "Hey, man, what's happenin'?"

"Well, I just told Larry and so I'm telling you. I'm keeping the album for Twentieth."

I was stunned and didn't know what to say. "Russ, I gotta go to the bathroom, I'll be right back." I dropped the phone and splashed cold water on my face. I looked at myself in the mirror. *He's keeping the album! The album he doesn't really hear and doesn't really want!*

I finally came back to the phone and rose up on it. "What are you talking about, Russ? We just made a deal with Clive Davis."

"Well, that's too bad because I'm keepin' the album."

I was on the edge of the bed, trying to keep my head on and think straight. "Russ? I mean, you said you didn't even like the album."

"Don't matter. I'm keepin' it."

"Fine. *You* tell Clive Davis he can't have it."

"I will."

And he did.

This was, as you might imagine, a major blow to Larry and me.

As he said he would, Russ Regan released the album on Twentieth Century, and, of course, even though he didn't hear it, it took off like a vertical rocket. His radio promotion front man, José, who, you remember,

also hadn't been able to hear it, took the album out on the road to promote to radio stations and came back singing a new tune. Now he was
predicting we couldn't help but hit big.

José said he became a believer when he saw how women reacted to my
voice. "You don't know what you have," he said to Russ. "There's something about Barry White's voice. Every woman who hears this album falls
in love with it and him."

Literally overnight, I became the label's biggest-selling artist. For the
first time I realized the true power of my voice. I became known as the
Maestro, not so much for leading the orchestra as leading *the way.* I began
to understand what it was that women were hearing and liked so much. It
wasn't just my music and narration, and it wasn't just the deep-voiced,
pure soul and vision of its creator. Surely there had been deep-voiced
singers before—people like Isaac Hayes and Lou Rawls. However, when I
sang, I didn't just celebrate a sound, I related to specific things in my songs
in a way that made everyone want to hear what it was I had to say. My
songs were positive, original, and *real,* and of course always sensitive to the
emotional feelings of men and women in love. They told real stories of
love and dealt with sex on an emotional level of depth that became the
essence of Barry White. "I've Got So Much to Give," "I've Found Someone," and "I'm Gonna Love You Just a Little More, Baby" all came off that
first solo album. They defined me as the newest pop icon of romantic perfection, not only in America but around the world.

To this day, when I write a song, I can hear the melody, the special
lyrics, and the dynamic arrangement—each distinctive and all at once.
That's the first part of the magic. The second is mixing it all together to
make a sound that works like, well, like an elixir of love. I'll hum a melody
into a cassette, beat out the drum part on my leg, and know immediately if I
have the makings of a new Barry White song. I don't follow the so-called
rules of chorus-verse-chorus because I don't *know or care* about those rules.
My dear friend and musician/producer Jack Perry says I hear music backward, because so often I'll write a chorus, followed by a verse, when it's "supposed to" be the other way around. I do it this way because I can't read music. Put a sheet music copy of "Love's Theme" in front of me without the

title and offer me a billion dollars to identify the song, and the money will stay with you. You see, "reading music" is the white man's invention. *Feeling* music, that's *my* heritage. In that sense, you could say I have a phono-graphic memory.

With the suc-cess of my solo al-bum, for the first time I began to realize my true *power* as an artist. How-ever, another kind of feeling emerged as well. I didn't talk about it to anybody, but something in my head went off like a set of flashing police lights. "What am I supposed to do now? Which way am I supposed to talk, to walk, now that I'm a star?" You don't think about these things un-til you become one. Then, when your dream comes true, you need to be prepared for the grand awakening. All I can tell you about it and all you really need to know on the subject is this. The dream is great. The life is better.

BY THE WAY, it wasn't until three years later that I finally found out what went down that morning when Russ decided he wasn't going to let the album go. I happened to be having lunch one afternoon with Spence Berland, a dear friend of mine and a critic for *Record World,* a trade publi-cation at the time. Anyway, we were sitting at the table when Spence said, out of nowhere, "That Russ Regan's a lucky son of a bitch."

"What do you mean, Spence?"

"You know, when he made the decision to keep your first solo album that time."

"I don't know what you're talking about."

Spence smiled and then told me "the rest of the story." The same night Larry made the deal with Clive Davis, Russ, Spence, and some others from the label were at a party for the DeFranco Family. Elton John happened to be there. Someone mentioned my album to Elton and played Russ's copy of the dub and he, Elton, supposedly went crazy over it. So much so, he took it home with him that night. It was on the strength of Elton's incredibly strong reaction that Russ rethought his decision. He figured if Elton liked it that much, it must have something, even if he, Russ, didn't hear it himself!

As soon as I had enough new material for a second Love Unlimited album, I paid a visit to Mike Maitland, Russ Regan's former boss at UNI, where the girls were still signed. Maitland and I didn't hit it off very well, and the next time we spoke, over the phone, he told me he was not inclined to do a lot of promotion for the girls' new album. This is the oldest and saddest story in the music business. Once they have hit artists, they move them down the food chain to make way for the next "big thing," and let the established talent sell on the memory of their previous hits for as long as they can before they fade.

I wasn't about to have any of it. I'd put too much time, blood, and tears into my career, and Love Unlimited, to let some record company executive arbitrarily dictate our future.

Right then and there I hung up the phone and went up to Maitland's office. I confronted him, *demanding* the outright release of the girls so I could move them over to Twentieth.

He proved to be far less a problem than I anticipated. "Fine," Mike said. "I don't want the group anyway. I'll give you their immediate release." With that, he picked up the phone and dialed his lawyers. Even before he hung up, I was on another phone with Russ Regan, making a deal with him for Love Unlimited. Yes, he'd played a little down and dirty with me in the past, but as I saw it, if he was the devil in disguise, at least it was a disguise I knew.

"Russ," I said, "Love Unlimited is yours if you want them."

"You can get me Love Unlimited?" he said, sounding surprised and excited.

"I sure can. I've already got their next album recorded and ready for release. It's called *Under the Influence of Love.*"

"Well, I want it, I want it . . ."

"Great," I said. "It's going to cost you ninety thousand dollars."

Without hesitation he said, "You have a deal."

I next called Larry Nunes, and then went to pick up the girls. We all then went over to Russ Regan's office, where the contracts were already drawn up and awaiting signature. Regan never even heard the album when he made the deal. That's how much he wanted them.

It was a whole new ballgame, one in which I was calling all the plays. Russ then turned me on to two of the best managers in the business—his way, I guess, of trying to reassure me that this time I'd really be protected. Their names were "Symphony" Sid Garris and George Grieff, and they were indeed very canny players. Both of them loved my work and wanted to represent me. I checked them out with Larry Nunes, who said they were okay, which was good enough for me. "Symphony" Sid, a Capricorn who'd been a legend on New York radio, would eventually become my conductor.

SHORTLY AFTER *Under the Influence of Love,* Love Unlimited's second album (and the first for Twentieth), was released, it became the first all-female album in the label's history to go Top 5 *in the crossover, mainstream pop charts!*

Now I'd given Russ Regan two of the hottest acts of the day, Barry White and Love Unlimited, and I still wasn't running at top speed.

I gave him another call. "Hey, man, I have this idea to cut an orchestra album." I've always had a great love for instrumentals, which comes from my mother, who used to play Bach, Beethoven, Brahms, and all the masters for me on her piano, which instilled in me a love of the sound of purely instrumental music.

I could hear his exasperation come huffing through the phone. "Aw, now, come on, Barry, you're just taking advantage!"

"That's what I want, Russ."

"You're crazy! It'll never sell. Nobody wants an instrumental."

"With the album that I'm envisioning, I think we can create a new market. I'm gonna cut an album with a full orchestra, and that's the way it's going to be!"

"You're just taking advantage of your record company, because you've got some clout now!"

"You're not going to know what I'm talking about until you hear it on record, Russ. And even then you might not get it. It seems to me we've been down this path before, haven't we?"

Russ sighed, and that's when I knew he knew he'd given in. "Okay, okay, I'm not going to say no. Just tell me one thing. What do you plan on calling *this* group?"

"The Love Unlimited Orchestra!"

"NOW YOU SEE, THAT'S WHAT I MEAN! IF ANYTHING, YOU SHOULD CALL IT THE BARRY WHITE ORCHESTRA. THE GIRLS ALREADY HAVE THAT NAME!"

"I know. Those three ladies of Love Unlimited are so dear to me I want to name my orchestra after them."

"What's your first single going to be?"

"One I was going to put on their new album. Instead I want to release it as the Love Unlimited Orchestra's first single. 'Love's Theme.'"

"OH MY GOD!"

IN 1973 THE Love Unlimited Orchestra's "Love's Theme" became something of an anthem in every disco in the world, and was on its way to being one of the biggest-selling instrumentals of all time. And oh, yes, Russ Regan, the man who "couldn't hear it," was named by *Record World* as the Executive of the Year, based on the success of Barry White, Love Unlimited, and the Love Unlimited Orchestra!

Still, even as I was enjoying my ride atop the charts, I could hear the whispers in the hallways of Twentieth Century Records about how I was one *lucky* fellow. What am I going to come up with next? they kept wondering, skepticism in the voices of those brave enough to ask me to my face.

My answer was always the same. "I'm coming up with Barry White," I'd say, hardly able to hold myself from laughing.

A few months later Russ Regan himself asked me what the name of my next album was going to be. I was ready.

"*Stone Gon'*. Wait until you hear it."

Even as I was busy writing and recording that album, I was getting the Love Unlimited Orchestra ready for its second album, *White Gold,* and putting the finishing touches on Love Unlimited's third album, *Love Unlimited in Heat. Heat* yielded a hit single, "I Belong to You," that went immediately to number 1. In 1974 I had *four albums*—mine, two of the orchestra's, and Love Unlimited—on the charts at the same time, along with a half-dozen singles.

WHILE I WAS cutting the track "Satin Soul" for the Love Unlimited Orchestra *White Gold* album, Glodean and I decided to get married.

After much thought, I decided I felt ready to try it again. I was a different Barry White now from the little boy who'd married Mary at such a young age. My relationship to Glodean was unique in so many ways. Perhaps most significant was that we'd met under professional circumstances and were producer/singer and friends first before we became lovers. This meant that Glodean knew not only what I was about but who I really was. She wasn't one of the neighborhood girls who always thought every real guy was a gang-banger, and every gang-banger was a real guy. She was far too elegant and sensitive to be impressed with any of that. As for me, I'd done a lot of growing up since my teenage relationship and marriage to Mary. I was no longer the jealous, insecure, primitive soul who separated himself from true love by false barriers such as pedestals so high no woman could ever hope to mount them. And whereas Mary thought my music was a great waste of time, an interference with the business of my real life, Glodean only knew me as a musician, to whom music meant everything. And she could sing! She was the perfect realization of my feminine side, the literal and figurative other half of me, the leading lady of the great romance plays around which I built so many of my love songs. Mary had been an unattainable fantasy, someone who sent me to the land of music in search of inspiration, while Glodean was the real thing, a woman who inspired me to make my own music. In her I had found someone with whom I could truly share the harmonies of love that played through the rhythms of my life.

However, before our actual wedding could take place, there was the not-so-little matter of finalizing my divorce from Mary and finding a permanent resolution for what had become a difficult issue between us, the ongoing question of custody. Although we had an agreement to share the children, she had decided to do battle over issues like the amount of child support she felt she needed, and hired a very tough attorney. Of all my children, only Barry, Jr., was already living with me full time. The others, Darryl, Lanese, and Nina, were with Mary during the week, while I had them on weekends. I wanted all the children to be together and felt I could provide a better home for them. I hired a young, eager lawyer of my own by the name of Ned Shankman, a partner in an up-and-coming Los Angeles law firm. Although we tried very hard to, Mary's side was not interested in settling, and we wound up going to trial. Just before it was to begin, with the help of my lawyer, we were finally coming to terms. I was eager to avoid putting the children through this, so I just agreed to give Mary ten thousand dollars a month—five for her, the other five for the children—and continue to share custody on a weekday-for-her, weekend-for-me basis. The judge said I didn't have to pay nearly that much, but to me, it wasn't about the law, it was about my children. By now my music was on the radio and the charts, and Mary and I felt the children were surely entitled to a piece of my action. I also bought them all a house near Larry Nunes's, in Encino, as far away from the ghetto as I could get them, and paid all the taxes on it so they could all be assured of a decent place to live. It may sound like a lot, but I could afford it. Besides, it was, quite honestly, a relief to be out of a courtroom as well as that marriage.

ONCE THAT WAS ALL SETTLED, Glodean and I were ready to tie the knot. We decided to keep it simple, and quietly flew to Las Vegas for a ceremony that was performed in a small chapel. We wanted to keep the rhythm of our romance right. Nevertheless, upon our return, Russ Regan and Twentieth Century Records insisted on throwing us a huge wedding reception at the Century Plaza Hotel built on the old back lot of the film studio. We made a quick appearance there, just long enough for Linda and Dede to tease me, saying things like, "Now that you're married, Uncle Barry, you have to find husbands for us!"

Glodean and I then headed for the one place we preferred to be when we were not in the studio or out on the road—*home with our children*. Glodean brought two children of her own into the mix. Then, not long after we were married, we had a baby girl of our own we named Shaherah, bringing our live-in total to four. That's where I've always found my true peace. Not in nightclubs, or hanging out with a bunch of people, or throwing big parties. I'm a homebody person by nature, Virgo with Capricorn rising, moon in Cancer. I'm a romantic at heart and prefer to stay out of the social mix, remaining close to the ones I love instead.

I willingly gave up touring during the peak of each summer season to be able to spend that precious time with all the children. It was the only way for me to be with my kids when they weren't either in school all day or with Mary and at the same time feel good about devoting so much of the rest of the year working on my music.

Glodean and I usually took the kids to Hawaii during the summer, as a kind of reward, because the rest of the year, believe me, they had to walk a hard line. They were taught to behave, do their schoolwork, and take care of their daily chores. And they had to do it all without me around every minute to guide them through the rough patches. This was my way of showing them a tangible reward for being good kids.

To me, this is what trying to have a successful career and family are all about—the endless trade-offs, compromises, and impossible odds that stack up against the attempt at being a star, a father, and a husband all at the same time.

ONE FALL DAY not long after Glodean and I got married, Russ came over to the studio, pulled me aside, and said he had something he wanted to give me. He reached in his pocket and took out a royalty check made out to Barry White for one million dollars. "Barry," he said proudly, "you are the franchise!"

"Give the money to Larry," I said, appreciative to be sure, but not wanting my concentration broken. When recording, it doesn't make any difference if someone wants to give me a single red rose or a seven-figure check, all my focus is on only one thing. The studio is my temple, and the music I create in it, sacred.

NEXT CAME THE OPPORTUNITY to do the score for the remake of the classic movie *King Kong*. Dino De Laurentiis's son heard one of my tracks and personally flew out from New York City to ask me to cut the film's theme song. That record, "King Kong's Theme," served as my entrée to movies, for me one of the great kicks of this business. And a long-lasting one at that. This past year, twenty years after *King Kong* came out, the film *Edtv* featured my version of Sly Stone's "Thank You."

Also in 1974, I embarked on my first world tour. What a trip, in every sense of the word! For the first time I was able to see with my own eyes a world that had only existed in school books, newspapers, and on the TV news. I'd come from being a nobody on the streets of South Central L.A. to a face recognized in foreign countries by a whole new audience for my music I hadn't even realized I had. The world seemed so different to me now, a place as vast and endless as the universe of music that had given me the opportunity to make this trip. I was thrilled and exhilarated by it all, as were the girls, who giggled and shopped and gawked and carried on like kids on a day trip with their favorite teacher to their most wondrous field of dreams.

Oh, yes, life had gotten so much sweeter for me! I was bigger than I ever dreamed I would be. I'd succeeded in lifting myself out of the mean streets by way of the big beat. I'd left behind forever the dead-end world of gang-bangers, muggers, and killers. And I was no longer this big, lovable dude whom everybody liked but who hadn't really *done* anything. Now it was my time to howl, and I'd turned on the world with the sound of my success!

I'd come to a place beyond the realm of so many others who get into music just to get girls or use it like a whore, make lots of money, to sleep late and party all night, and to work as little as possible. In my world making music was and still is as pure and vital as the pulse that throbs through my heart. The very thought of misusing my gift is, to me, the true definition of sin.

Now, I had become the man I was destined to be, a first-class citizen of the world of popular music.

I was, finally, Barry White.

SEVEN

I Am, You Are, and It Is

"Practice What You Preach"

Yeah, there's something wrong with me.
Every time I'm alone with you,
You keep talkin' 'bout you lovin' me,
Hey, babe, your foreplay just blows my mind!
So, why don't we stop all the talkin' girl?
Why don't we stop wastin' time?
I've had my share of lovers, some say I'm damn good.
And if you think you can play me out, baby, I wish that you would
'Cause you keep tellin' me this and tellin' me that.
You say once I'm with you I'll never go back.
You say there's a lesson that you wanna teach,
Well, here I am baby, practice what you preach.

YOU SHOULD INDEED *practice what you preach. When it comes to love, sometimes it's better if you stop talking about it and just do it. If you're thinking something's wrong, it might very well be that there is. But if you're thinking something is right, I know surely it must be so.*

Ladies, be cautious in your selection of men. Don't get into a relationship first and then complain that there is nothing you can do that's going to change your man. Know who he is going in and make sure you like what you know. And men, be yourself. Don't go promising what you can't deliver. Don't say in the heat of the moment you'll buy them a washer-dryer, a big house, a new car, furs, jewelry, all of that which you think will make you a better man in their eyes. Don't try to put a price tag on your love. Don't diminish your emotions in that way. You will have done nothing more than helped achieve the opposite. You'll have taken your eye off the love ball. Offer who you are, not what you might or might not have one day farther down the line. You'll both be better off for it, I guarantee.

Now don't misunderstand me. There is a power and beauty to seduction. My music is all about that seduction. This is my thing, and probably yours as well. However, the point of commitment is that it isn't about things but about people. Be honest, know who you are, and be willing to show yourself that way. Seduce, yes, but know that you will still be there the next morning, and so will your lover, in the cool light of the day that surely always follows the hot glow of the night before.

There will be times when your man has to be alone. Don't take this as a rejection. Let him wander through the solitude of his own mind. Let that thinking process take place. Let the mind expand, and the emotions will likely come along for this ride. When he is ready for you, you'll know. Being alone does not necessarily mean being apart, any more than being apart has to mean being alone.

Men, don't try to fool yourself, because that's the only person you will be fooling. If you aren't true to yourself, you will wind up exposing yourself in so many ways before the very eyes of the one you want most to impress. Pay attention to each other, and you will learn everything you ever need to know about what it will be like to be in love together. Neither one will ever have to ask any questions about it. Instead, you will lay it out in beautiful and bold behavior.

Ladies, you have the advantage, because you know how to listen better than men. We're too busy listening to our own egos. Get through that, and you will find the inner soul of your mate.

Remember, she wants to listen. She wants to get next to you, know you, get into your soul. It's called being in love. Never, never treat or talk to a lady like she isn't someone special. There really is no other way. Remember, please—there is nothing in this world worth having if you don't have a man or a woman to share it with.

·   ·   ·

I WAS THE Barry White the world loved, but I was still me, of course, the same Barry White who'd sold toys, who'd gang-banged in South Central, who'd gone to jail and from there on to glory. What the world saw was *one part* of Barry White, the man who made music. I was, and still am, several Barry Whites, part public figure, part private man, part lyrical riffer, part philosophical spiritualist.

If I am writing a song, then I am Barry White the songwriter. When I need someone to take what he has created and shape it for recording, I am Barry White the produeer. When I need someone to put it all together in sync—the voices, the orchestra, the chorus, and so on, I am Barry White the arranger. When I need someone whose voice carries my combined

efforts, I am Barry White the singer.

Each of these skills is an art form unto itself, and each requires an individual artist to do it justice. Each has to work with all the others to help, assist, and develop who he is and what he has. Each has to bring something new and different to the table. And each is a part of me.

I am also Barry White the husband, Barry White the father, and Barry White the son. I am Barry White the fantasy to my fans all over the world. And I am Barry White the friend for those to whom music may be the farthest thing from their minds.

The combined aspects of all my varied facets add up to Barry White the *man,* multi facets of the same diamond soul. There is an expression that goes "Out of many there is one." How true—in spite of all the Barry Whites I have defined above, the many people I know whom I work with, socialize with, create with, live with, and love with all will tell you they know the same Barry White everyone else knows. This was true before I became famous and remains true to this day.

Because we are *all* many people within ourselves, and those many are all out of one. In that sense, each and every one of us is a god. I remember in church when they used to talk about how God was really three people—the Father, the Son, and the Holy Ghost—what they were really saying was "Out of many, one." I am aware of this, and it is the reason I work just as hard no matter what aspect of myself I am living in, at any given day, time, or place. It is also why I reject all these titles people seem to want to lay on me. I am no maestro, no guru, no icon of love. I am simply Barry Eugene White, one, always, and forever.

A man cannot be an icon. Love is a *power,* not a person. The only true icon is love, and that is at the top of the order of all of my priorities. If you have that, there is nothing other people can teach you that you don't already know about it and nothing else worth having. If you don't have love, then you have nothing.

Everybody wants love to do something for them. They want love to do this, they want love to do that. They want love to *fix* everything rather than *be* everything. Love may make you feel as if it's doing what you want, but in reality, you're kidding yourself. You have to manifest things you want to happen *through* love. How do you do that? To be able to love somebody, you've got to learn to be unselfish, whether you're a man or a woman. You must sacrifice that selfish part of yourself in order to see the effect take properly. That's what I believe a lot of men and women aren't really ready for, to take their individuality and carve it down the middle. Every part of your half is yours. Every part of the other half is hers or his. And that should be enough for the both of you. If she asks what you are holding back in that other half, and says that maybe some of it belongs to her, that's trouble. If she says thank you for giving me as much as you have, you're all right. What we offer of ourselves to each other, in our deeds, not our words, is the true measure of love. Remember that, and you will understand your partner so much better. Unfortunately, most of the time people who insist they are "in love" don't really know their own half at all, while insisting they get every piece of the other person's half, which is really his whole. They make the same mistakes over and over again. If you have a problem with your partner, it may very well be that *you* are the problem. You've got to be willing to look at all of it, to understand any of it. You've got to be ready, willing, and able to acknowledge who you are, and who he or she is, and what is happening between the two of you.

You have to show yourself truly naked; I don't mean without clothes, I mean with your feelings exposed, ready to be shared by the other, your *true* feelings, no matter what they may be. The opposite of this is a form of lying, which is the cancer of love. Achieving this kind of truth is a higher form of love than the greeting-card level we've all had forced down our throats since we were too young and innocent to know better.

Men, stop trying to sell yourself with promises of material goods you won't be able to deliver. That's not love, that's falsehood to win her body. Her mind will never accept the lie of those idle promises you made just to get her. Don't be a bully and force your will onto another for your own selfish gains. Don't pretend to be the best husband or wife in the world. Instead, try to be the best husband or wife *you can be.* Strive for that higher awareness. Once you understand this, you will understand yourself and your lover so much better, on a higher and more profound level.

Love is not easy on any level—easy to find, easy to sustain, easy to give up. "I'm in love with you" really means "I'm in love with you *today.*" What is truly sinful to me is that our society sets us up from day one to believe just the opposite, that whomever or whatever you're in love with will automatically love you back for as long and as intensely as you'd like. All these fairy tales do nothing more than ruin our lives. Fathers telling sons men never cry. *Of course they cry.* All men cry. Tragically, some pay a self-inflicted price for showing that emotion because they think it's wrong.

Each of us has the ability to face the truth of our lives. Instead of making idle promises of a lifetime, why not say instead to each other that you may not know how long this is going to last, but as long as it does, you will both use your power to make it as great as it can be. The real romantic vow is the promise to leave room for change! Not necessarily the way you want that change to come but accepting whatever changes in each of you as it comes.

And I mean change in every way. Beauty is something that is both a blessing and a curse. Don't depend on the power of your beauty, ladies, to get things. External beauty doesn't last forever. Depend instead on the power of the beauty of your knowledge.

The power in my music comes from the way I try to deliver what I believe is the power of love. All of my songs essentially give out the same message, from me to you—I am, you are, and it is.

This is the philosophy I live by. *I am, you are, and it is.* I am a god. You are a god. We have the power to create, and we have the power to destroy, even life itself. I've certainly created life with my children. I've never taken a life, but I know I could do it if I had to protect them. "It" is what we cannot see that we cannot control, that affects us every day of our lives. "It" goes where it wants to go and does what it wants to do. It is the ultimate linking force, the ether of our spirit. "It" is time. "It" is awesome, pure, and powerful. Hurricanes, earthquakes, the passage of events, falling in and out of love, these are some of "It," that force of nature which is just as strong and godlike as we are.

I am. Never forget this power you possess. We try to make things happen but the most important thing to understand is that we don't own nature and therefore *nothing is guaranteed.* Because of this simple truth, a lot of man-made things are temporary, hollow, and false, and don't impress me very much. Trees are real. *They* impress me. Grass is real. The ocean is real. A bee sucking nectar from a plant, that's real. The feeling I have for the woman I love is real. These are essential commodities of life, things I choose to deal with, things I *believe in.*

Still, we call each other man and woman, not god and goddess, and this is a good thing. It keeps us grounded and rational. Take the fairy-tale, self-congratulatory nature of show business, the profession I happen to be in. The Grammy Awards, for instance, come and go every year, and the winners who are celebrated are as quickly forgotten as the losers. I've seen artists actually *cry* because they didn't win. As far as I'm concerned, it's a *privilege* to win *or* lose. Anyway, the real reward is the man or woman who comes up to me and says, "Barry, I got married to 'I Can't Get Enough.' We *made love* to that record." Now *that's* an award.

I am, you are, and it is!

Being honest, carrying myself a certain way, being aware of how I speak to people, understanding that when I write a love song I'm saying things to *individuals* who are *listening* to me, avoiding the hype of being sold as the next big mack daddy, these are all essential philosophies of Barry White.

Because of that, I have an amazingly sensitive bullshit detector. When it goes off, I say to myself here is one of those people who is trying to take something from me that doesn't belong to them, someone who wants to steal my heart, my mind, my money, or my soul.

My shows are an extension of my personal philosophy of life. No frills, no fireworks going off in the sky, none of that. What you get is Barry White, in front of a microphone, telling you how it is from the inside. Same deal, onstage and off. I don't drink, I don't fool around with women, I don't gamble, and I don't jive. I make my music and perform it, and because enough people like it, I am privileged to be able to do a lot of other things. If I see a child starving, I can feed it. If I see a woman who has fallen, I can help lift her up. If I see a brother in trouble, I can help him out. If I see an injustice, I can try to correct it. If I have children, I can be a good parent. Speaking of which, being Barry White the father is just about the most important thing in my life.

I know grown people who remember one thing about their parents—that they were never hugged by either one. Every time I see my children, the first thing I do is hug and kiss them. I want my kids to know how important they are to me and that I'm there for them, *with love in my heart.* I don't tell them I'm *in love* with them, because I want them to grow up understanding the difference and being able to live their lives that way. I must set a good example in my own home, because kids know the difference between "putting up a front" and true love between their parents. My children know that I love them, that I will always love them. They are secure in their self-image, because I am secure in mine. I treat my children the way I see them, understanding they will do whatever they want; they can wreak havoc in our lives until they get old enough and know what they want are right things. How will they know what's right and what's wrong? *Because they're little gods and goddesses who will one day grow up to be big gods and goddesses, imbued with the power and the knowledge that I and their mothers have bestowed on them.*

This is so important, because our paths are chosen at such an early age, if we are to believe the media and sometimes even our own eyes. Every day we see on the news how this twelve-year-old killed that twelve-year-old, or this ten-year-old raped that ten-year-old, or this seven-year-old took a gun to that seven-year-old, and so on. Parents today do *not* know how to raise their kids, because they weren't raised properly themselves. They don't know how to make a real commitment to each other by getting married and taking the responsibility for the lives they bring into the world. They don't know how to commit to their jobs, they don't know how to commit to their welfare and security. The ability to make a commitment remains as crucial as anything in life, no matter what that commitment may be.

Once I commit to someone or something, be it my lady or raising our children, I see it as a spiritual contract that must not and cannot be broken. In that sense, I will always have the last word in what happens to me. Practice what you preach, practice what you teach. To hell with Maggie's farm; get your own spread and be the true and only master of your character and your fortune, your future and your fate.

Out of all you receive in your life, it is important to understand what it is you actually have. Let's say it's a gold mine. It isn't any good to you unless you know how to turn it into something of value. And now, let's say that gold mine is another person. That gold right up under your nose could be a beautiful woman, but if you're so busy waiting for the glitter to materialize without going down and bringing it out, you'll wait a very long time. Sooner or later some other man will come along and push you aside, ready, willing, and able to work for the rewards he knows will come.

Sometimes it comes down to a moment as simple as if you greet me with a smile, that's the way I will greet you, and continues all the way to if you want to make this marriage work, so do I. Remember, if people treat you badly, if your wife is not into it, if your kids don't seem to want to be with you, it could very well be your fault as much as if not more than theirs. Selfishness and arrogance somehow always seem to go together in situations like these. Look to yourself for the answers, not to others for excuses or rationales.

I know who I am, and if you know who you are, let's get to know one another the right way, without putting the game on each other. Women always tell me they're surprised how easy it is to talk to me. I tell them that's because I never run a game on them. I prefer to deal in truth, not deception. Trust, not trickery. Decency, not deception. Love, not lust; this is where I come from. This is why my music is always so positive. I am in control of my creative force. I see a world of beauty and perfection, and I strive through my music to spread that vision, to help make this planet we call home a better, more desirable place for us to love one another, to procreate, and to keep our spirits renewed.

When I pass from this mortal life, I want to be buried in the ocean. Why? To return to the place from which all of life once came. I want to be wrapped in a simple shroud and placed within the great natural underwater peace that engulfs so much of this otherwise troubled and turbulent planet.

EIGHT

THE TRUE AMERICAN DREAM

"LOVE AIN'T EASY"

We're so perfect for each other,
Still, you have some doubt
You're holding back your love, girl . . .

Just in case it don't work out
Girl, we know love ain't easy,
Something no one can deny
But we will know if we can make it
We won't know girl, not until we try
We won't know until we try.

T HIS IS A SONG *about the fear of trying a relationship and not knowing if it will last. It's as much a love song as any of my others, only it looks at love from a slightly different, perhaps more realistic, angle. Failing in a relationship is nothing to be ashamed of. It simply means you gave it a try and it didn't work. Not being able to pick yourself up and move on with your life is the only real tragedy.*

How can you ever say to someone I love you today and mean it as I will love you forever? Sometimes a couple's time together just runs out. One or both change. Things don't feel like they used to. It may not be a major or tangible thing, but when it happens, believe me, you know. You see everything a whole lot differently. You may not be a conniver, a game runner, or even someone who has to have a lot of lovers. Sometimes people just change—their perspectives, needs, and desires change. And a lot of the time the relationship or the other person resists this change. Some people can flow and adapt, and some can't.

A lot of the time, couples will break up because of a third party—another woman or another man. Maybe the thrill of sex is over, or they discover that living together doesn't work for them, or they're just not ready or suited to devote the rest of their lives to this one other person. It is no sin, and no crime, moral or otherwise, unless the other person takes it as a violation of a specific pledge of faith, which would be unfair, since nobody has a crystal ball to predict the future. I'm not saying that it's all right to cheat on your partner. I don't think anybody goes into a relationship with that desire. It's just that when two

people get together, they are taking a chance on the other person and them-
selves. If it doesn't work, for whatever reason, it's really better to move on and
look to the future rather than pointing fingers and dwelling in the guilt-
ridden past. No one is perfect. People change, or they make mistakes, or their
relationship runs its natural course. I believe it is better to enjoy the good times
while you have them than to try to preserve happiness like it was deposited in
the bank for some future use.

People who don't see this waste so much time chasing a dream they can
never live out in real life. The only solution is to love as hard and as sincerely as
you can, for as long as it lasts, and to allow the natural time span of that love
to flow completely. It may last a day, it may very well last a lifetime. But for
however long it runs, enjoy it to the fullest capacity, and you will have few re-
grets for having done so, no matter what the outcome.

· · ·

BECOMING A FIRST-CLASS CITIZEN in the world of popular music
opened doors for me I didn't even know existed. I am living the *true*
American dream. I've been privileged by my special gift for music to be
able to lift myself out of the dead-end nightmare of the ghetto to a place
somewhere on the other side of the great world's rainbow of success. Because of it, I've seen some extraordinary things in my life and met some
incredible people.

I had the rare privilege of getting to meet the greatest fighter of all
time, the Golden Child, Muhammad Ali. I remember when I was a
youngster watching him on TV the day he announced he would no longer
be known by his slave name, Cassius Clay, but from that moment on he
would be Muhammad Ali. Years later when I met him, I told him how
much that had always meant to me, both as a black man and as a citizen of
this world.

Muhammad and I became good friends, and I've always loved his
childlike innocence as much as his wise man's knowledge and judgment.
There are men and there are gods. He is truly one of the rarest of living
legends—he is both.

Once, during his championship days, I sat with him in Las Vegas before a fight. He was talking about something, all light and funny, and then suddenly, without warning, he got into his warrior head. His eyes shifted and took on the look of a very sleek and dangerous cat. I saw that same look on his face after he destroyed his opponent. I get a similar kind of intensity when I am working at my art in the studio or alone by myself working deep into the night. He was awesome when he left the dressing room and went into the ring, as he was for every fight.

He's come to so many of my concerts and still drops by my house at all hours of the day and night. He'll wake up my kids at four o'clock in the morning because he wants to show them magic tricks. I've also spent time with him in a gym down in Miami, where he liked to discuss new ideas for business. Some of them were pretty good, most weren't. One time he told me he wanted to build a hotel in the ghetto of Miami.

I said, "Muhammad, where's your security budget?"

"What do you mean?"

"If you build a hotel in the ghetto, you're going to need a major security budget. Not for you, not for me, but for the sheets, the towels, for everything that has your name on it and isn't nailed down!"

He looked at me like a little boy and said, "I never thought of that!"

•   •   •

I HAVE MET so many others whose precious gifts have enriched all our lives—great men and women, some of whom I've known personally, others, like Nelson Mandela, through their enormous contributions to our world. Some memories I have connected to my music are funny and warm, like the time I was told by a good friend that the only music Ted Kennedy plays on his private yacht is that of yours truly, Barry White. This still knocks me out!

I actually got to meet the senator once, at an industry luncheon. Mr. Kennedy was being honored for his part in the long-standing and ongoing battle to protect the copyrights of writers and artists. I was introduced to him and we hit it right off. Afterward we rode down together in an elevator, surrounded by Secret Service agents, and in those brief seconds the senator confirmed the rumor. "Mr. White," he said, "I'm one of your biggest admirers. I'm happy you could make it to the luncheon, and by the way, I can't tell you how much I love your music. I listen to it all the time!"

ALTHOUGH I DIDN'T actually produce him, I *did* get to help a young Michael Jackson in the 1980s, before he became a superstar. At the time, CBS was against his making a new album he wanted to call *Off the Wall*. They didn't believe he could make it as a solo act and insisted he keep the Jackson Five intact.

It wasn't only the label that was against the idea. His family didn't go for it either, all of which hurt him on a very deep and personal level. When he needed someone to talk to about all of it, he decided I was the one.

I'd first met the Jacksons in 1975, in Los Angeles at the Century Plaza Hotel, where they were rehearsing for an industry convention. Jermaine and I were immediately drawn to each other. I didn't learn until later that he was a huge Barry White fan. We hooked up, started hanging out together, and eventually the Jacksons bought homes in the San Fernando

Valley near each other and me. We camped out together on overnight fishing trips and became quite close. Later that same year Jermaine's wife, Hazel, and Glodean were pregnant at the same time, and went through that whole experience together.

Michael felt I was one of the few people he could trust because he knew that no matter what, I would be honest with him. He loved the fact that I was afraid of nothing and nobody, that I was my own man, something he aspired to be.

When he ran into his trouble at the label, I was the one he called. I told him to come over, and that night we talked for five and a half hours about the situation. He cried throughout, because, he said, they'd hurt his feelings so badly. All he wanted was a fair shot at a solo career. I decided to try to help him get it.

First, though, I gave him a long lecture on the responsibility he had to make sure he felt to his own music. I told him he had to work to get the album he wanted made, *no matter what,* because he'd never know if he could be a hit as a solo unless he went ahead and gave it his best shot. I finally convinced him not to listen to anyone or anything but his own calling.

He said he wanted Quincy Jones to produce the album, and I told him to go out and get him.

Michael started coming over every day, wanting to learn the secret of how I'd gotten to control my own music and publishing, the production of my own records, and therefore my own destiny. I explained to him the difference between us, how he believed he was a pure "artist" while I was always aware *and* wary of the real world. I tried to educate him, so that he could understand how the music world operated, to be a little more of a businessman and a bit less the temperamental artist.

The next thing I knew, he managed to make *Off the Wall,* produced by the great Quincy Jones. I listened to it and heard pieces of so many of my arrangements, which I took only as a compliment. Not only that, but Michael went on to become one of the savviest players in the music business, owning a good piece of the Beatles' catalog and a lot of other publishing as well, and taking complete control over the making of his albums. It's a good feeling to know that you've reached somebody and helped show him the way.

I DID HAVE the great privilege to meet President Clinton's secretary of commerce, the late Ron Brown, an appointment that made so many black people happy and proud. One time when I was invited to Washington, D.C., to perform at a fund-raising affair, I happened to run into him backstage. Of course, I knew who he was, but what knocked me out was that he knew who I was. When he told me he liked my music and was a fan, I looked at him, smiled, and said softly, "And I am one of yours, sir." He was a great man we lost way, way too soon.

I met the legendary Joe Louis when he was a greeter at Caesars Palace, long after his days of glory had passed him by. His talent for winning, particularly against Max Schmeling, Hitler's pride and joy, gave black people in this country a huge boost of pride and self-esteem. In spite of his heroics on the world stage of athletics, in his own country Joe paid the heavy price of prejudice, and when he aged, his years of pummeling had left him weak and dependent. His problems with the government over taxes were an outrageous slap in the face to every black person in America. Whenever I meet history-bound old-timers like him, I try to learn from them the way they handled themselves in their prime and out of it. It's wondrous for me to see these men who *did it,* who were there, and to observe how the world reacts to their accomplishments. I was honored to shake Mr. Louis's hand, and, in spite of some of the bad things he fell victim to in his life, hoped he knew how much he was loved and appreciated by so many people of all colors and races in this country and around the world.

Another great fighter I got to know fairly well was "Marvelous" Marvin Hagler. I can especially relate to Marvin because of how he literally fought his way out of the penitentiary and into greatness. I used to go see him fight while he was still inside, down in Washington, D.C., and was amazed at his progress, how he used his skill and abilities to get himself out of jail and into the professional ring. I think his street-tough style of fighting always reminded me of my brother. He has what it takes to be a champion—not just talent, but also stamina, will, and the courage to overcome early hardship and misfortune. His is a true success story. Every time I go to Italy, where Hag now lives, I make it a point to try to catch up with him and spend a little time together.

I met a young heavyweight named Mike Tyson in Los Angeles, when we both happened to be staying at the Beverly Wilshire Hotel. He saw me in the lobby and went *off,* like a little kid, I guess because in so many ways he *was* a little kid. "Barry White! I love you, man! I grew up with your music! Come to the car and let me show you something!" He took me to his limo, opened the door, and my CDs were all over the backseat! I told him that I'd seen him fight many times, and he'd shown *me* some things as well.

I HAD THE EXTREME honor of seeing the Reverend Dr. Martin Luther King, Jr., speak in person at Wrigley Field in Chicago one time. He was so dynamic, it was an inspiring moment in my life I'll never forget. And of course there was the great Malcolm X.

I was still a boy when I almost got killed trying to meet Malcolm. I didn't know at the time that he was always heavily guarded. I learned a lot that day in Los Angeles when he came to town and everybody was looking to meet him. I had heard enough about him to want to make it my business to see him up close and in person. He was holding a rally at the mosque on 54th and Broadway, and when I first saw him there were about eight gentlemen dressed in black suits surrounding him. I cut right through the crowd and, when I was within maybe five or ten feet, stuck out my hand for him to shake. Before I knew it his people had grabbed me in such a way that I couldn't move. Of course they were doing what they had to do and had no way of knowing it was only youthful enthusiasm on my part that made me want to push forward and get up close to Malcolm. Once they realized I was all right, they let me shake the great man's hand. I felt both of his against mine, which is how he did it. I couldn't help but notice their incredible warmth. It was almost like a personal delivery of passion. And those amazing, piercing eyes.

"You look like a very smart young brother," he said, smiling. "What do you do?"

I told him I was going to school and then added, "Mr. X, it is really a pleasure meeting you." That was as close as I ever got to him, but it was enough for me to realize how humble he was, how real, and how inspirational. I'd seen him on television, and now I had touched him. To me, it was like touching greatness. I was, at that moment, inspired to reach for a new level of personal respect and fulfillment in my life. Today a magnificent painting of Malcolm X hangs in the living room of my home.

My success has given me a special type of freedom, and I feel it most clearly in the joy I experience meeting such living legends. They conduct their lives in a very specific way. I have had so many wonderful, *priceless* opportunities to meet *history* in the flesh, and these opportunities are what I consider one of the true privileges of fame.

I have, of course, also shared some great experiences with many wonderful and famous women, such as Congresswoman Maxine Waters. Maxine is my girl. She's a fighter for our cause, for black people to be recognized and treated as *people.* She is truly remarkable. I've worked with her often on fund-raisers, particularly when it came time to help rebuild South Central after some of the trouble of the 1990s. I think the best thing I can say about her is that she never reminded me of a politician, just somebody fighting for what she believes in, trying to do good for others.

In 1991 I was honored to be invited to her inauguration in Washington, D.C. What a fantastic experience.

And Oprah Winfrey. What a fabulous lady! I met Oprah when I did her show and had the best time imaginable. She made me feel very comfortable and did an excellent, classy, and elegant interview. She knows her business. She is, in my judgment, outstanding, as a person, as a woman, as a black woman. I'm very proud of her to this day. She is a shining light to *all* women, a great spark for men. She has taught people a lot through example and the experts she has on her show. She's a star to me.

S O M E M E M O R I E S I have connected to my music are funny and warm. And some are very sad, like my all-too-brief association with Marvin Gaye.

Ahh, Marvin. He summed up so much in one simple question: *"What's Goin' On?"* That remains one of my favorite songs, from one of my favorite albums. Marvin was a truly great singer, writer, musician, producer, and arranger. He could do it all. Even his album covers carried his creative mark, like the one with Marvin in his trench coat, in the rain, asking his most pivotal of questions.

Unfortunately, I couldn't get too up close and personal with Marvin, because of his lifestyle. He had a significant dark side. I always sensed that Marvin carried around a big hurt, things that stemmed from his childhood, particularly with his father, which he expressed in self-destructive ways designed to do him no good. In that way he reminded me a little of my brother, Darryl, whose own childhood struggles haunted him the rest of his life.

I knew a lot about Marvin from the street. The street will give you more information than any newspaper or magazine. I knew he had some demons and was fighting them. I don't judge him or anyone for what they needed to do with their lives. If it doesn't agree with me, I keep my distance and let others do their thing. Marvin was a troubled man, and that is why he and I were not closer to one another. He had done a song called

"Give Back My Mind," which always struck me as a plea from Marvin's soul that it wanted him to be healthier. It's sad to me that he'll never know how much I loved him, how I knew every song in his catalog from the time he started, and how proud for him I was that he accomplished as much with his music as he did.

As it happened, in 1984 the Friday before he died Marvin got in touch with Don Cornelius to try to find me. I had just come back from a tour in Israel, and as I was going through the Los Angeles airport, everyone was coming up and telling me how great this new album was going to be.

"What new album?" I asked.

"The one with you and Marvin." I didn't know what they were talking about, but I just said thanks. It wasn't until I got home that I saw in *Billboard* Marvin had announced I was going to produce his next album.

The next thing I knew the phone is ringing. Don Cornelius. I hadn't seen or spoken to Don in at least six months. "Chiefie," he said, which was what we called each other, "how you doin'?"

"Fine," I said.

We talked for a few seconds, and then he said, "B.W., somebody here wants to talk to you."

The next thing I knew, Marvin was on the phone. "Hey, B.W."

"What's happenin', Marvin?" I asked. I was so happy to hear his voice.

"Well, I've just been trying to get myself going," he said. "Trying to get to you, man."

"Yeah, I heard about that," I said, laughing.

"B.W., you got to produce my next album."

"Marvin," I said, "you're *insane!* You don't need a *producer!* That's the *last* thing you need. Now, if you want another mind and a set of good ears to take a shot at what songs you want to do, I think maybe I can help you. But I can never *produce* Marvin Gaye. *Marvin* is the only one that can produce Marvin."

"Okay, Barry," he said. "Can we get together and talk about it?"

"Sure."

"How's Monday?"

"Monday is great, Marvin."

"I'll be over your house about two."

"I'll be here."

"Fantastic, B.W." I could hear him smiling through the phone.

I looked forward to that meeting so much that the next day I started thinking about writing a song for the both of us to do together. By the time I went to bed Saturday night I was so excited I couldn't think about anything else.

I woke up Sunday morning to the phone ringing. I picked it up and somebody on the other side said, "Did you hear what happened?"

That's when and how I got the bad news. *Marvin Gaye was dead.*

People started calling one after the other to tell me. Hazel and Jermaine Jackson called, all broken up. He was their "Uncle Marvin." In this instance, Marvin actually *was* their uncle, because he'd married Anna, Hazel's auntie, Berry Gordy's sister.

Hazel, Glodean, Jermaine, and I arrived at the funeral early, so no one would see me there. I looked down at Marvin in his casket, bent over, kissed him on his beautiful face, and left.

His passing hit me so hard and deep. It broke my heart. He was looking to make an even bolder leap, to stretch, to work himself to a new level. Now he is gone forever. It is everybody's loss.

LARRY NUNES DIED in 1978, in his sleep, from a massive heart attack at the too-young age of forty-eight. When I heard this news, I felt as if half my world had gone with him. To this day, nobody has or ever will fill the personal and creative void he left in my life.

The first sign he was not, in fact, going to live forever, something I thought was a foregone conclusion, actually came two years before he died, in 1976, when Larry came over to my house to tell me something.

"I got to talk to you, Barry," he said. "I want to retire."

I was taken completely by surprise. "Why, man? We're on top of the world. We've got it all. Why would you want to walk away from that, Larry?"

His answer shocked and saddened me. "Because I'm ashamed, man."

His main problem, he told me, was a stubborn twenty-year gambling habit that had all but eaten him alive. He told me he once blew four and a half million dollars in one weekend in Las Vegas. Now, he said, his day of reckoning had finally come. During all the good years he'd never bothered to pay a single cent in taxes. Larry Nunes, the man who'd given me my big break in music, was now sitting in my house asking me for one hundred thousand dollars so he could afford to retire.

I wasn't going to let it happen like that. Without Larry Nunes there would have been no Barry White. The next morning I called a meeting at the Sunset Boulevard offices of Mo' Soul Records. The big boys from Mo' Soul's distribution company, Twentieth Century Records, were all there, the cats who'd become rich off of the good fortunes of this company. They were curious to know what was going down. I wasted no time telling them of Larry's plans.

"Oh, good, good . . ." they said among themselves, shaking their heads and rubbing their palms together. Their lack of compassion and the smell of their greed made me angry. I decided to play with them a little, to make sure they understood what this was all about.

"Larry wants a hundred thousand dollars as a retirement bonus."

No one said anything. I could tell they were frightened about having to pay out even a penny. I leaned into the table and chose my next words deliberately. "But you know, maybe he doesn't have that much coming. Maybe it should be more like forty, or maybe fifty."

Now they went crazy, thinking they were going to be able to get rid of him for even less. That's when I dropped the other, very expensive shoe on them.

"But you know what, guys? We can never properly repay Larry for all he's done for everyone in this room. That's why we're going to try to make some kind of proper demonstration of our gratitude and give him *a million dollars!*"

I turned to one of their accountants. "And you make sure he gets it."

I nodded my head to Larry, stood up, and said, "We're on our way, man."

After he retired, to settle his tax problems and still be able to keep some of that million dollars, he suggested I buy his house. "It's a fine one, Barry," he said, "a good home to raise children in." I gave him full market value, $140,000, and on top of that another $140,000 to find a place for himself in Sherman Oaks not far from the old house.

Larry's place turned out to be perfect for my family—the right size, in a good neighborhood, Sherman Oaks, right in the heart of the San Fernando Valley.

Once Glodean, the kids, and I moved in, I did a massive fix-up. There hadn't been children in this house for many years. I landscaped, added a basketball court, a big screening room, a billiards room, and of course a game room for the kids. I even had a waterfall put in. I kept a huge aquarium for myself and, as a housewarming gift, bought Glodean a baby tiger. Each of the children got his or her own dog.

I also bought the house and land directly above us, on the hill, and made it into a recording studio, to complete what would become, in effect, my North Hollywood compound, a creative sanctuary and a safe place to raise my family. I wanted my kids to be able to run free and play, with no one telling them they didn't belong or they had to go home. I wanted them to feel secure knowing the land they were standing on was *ours*.

And yet as much as we made it our own, I always felt in some ways like a fortunate caretaker. It was a good feeling to know that Larry Nunes had raised his kids in this house and now I was going to raise mine there as well.

HOWEVER, THE SADDEST of all my memories begins and ends with my brother, Darryl, and my mother. By the time Darryl was released from his too-long stretch in the pen in 1978, I'd already become a recording star with several hit records. I knew that my success had to mess his troubled head up even more. "What do you want to do, now that you're out?" I asked him, knowing how difficult it was going to be for him to try to get a job when the first thing anybody was sure to ask about was the thirteen years missing from his record. I offered to set him up in any business he wanted.

"All I want is a shoe shine stand, Burly" was his response. "'Course I ain't really into polishing shoes. The back room, that's where the action'll be."

I sighed. Always that criminal shit. "Burly, do you really think I can put my money into that and be associated with it?"

"Well, you asked me, man, and that's all I could think of."

Instead, I gave him a thousand dollars a week to do with what he wanted until the day he died. When I made that decision, I remember my accountant called and said I was giving Darryl too much. I went off on her so cold—she didn't have any idea what we'd been through as brothers, as a family.

"This is my brother and I'll give him all of my money if I want to!"

After that she never said another word about it. There are some lines you don't cross.

A couple of years later he finally came face to face with his own destiny over a silly incident that meant absolutely nothing more than trying to take petty advantage of another man. Darryl, you see, was killed over *change.*

He was living in a boardinghouse in South Central, and one of the other tenants asked him if he'd mind picking up some goods at the grocery store, as Darryl was going there anyway. He said okay and when he came back, the man accused Darryl of shortchanging him. Now *both* of them went crazy. The guy told Darryl he wanted the rest of his money, and when Darryl said there wasn't any the guy went and got his gun. Darryl asked him what that was for. "You're going to give me my money, *motherfucker!*" Understand, Darryl was thirty-seven, the other guy was sixty-seven, which didn't mean anything to either one of them. My brother was the kind of guy who if you pulled a gun on him you had to kill him or you were dead, 'cause he'd kill you with his bare hands. The guy shot three times, hit him only once, but straight through the heart. The coroner said the wound was so clean Darryl only bled a tablespoon of blood. I'm telling you that bullet had his *name* on it. It still rips me up inside to think that Darryl is gone. He was so young, so strong, and so full of life, his death took a hard piece out of me.

It killed my mother too, in a different way. Surely afterward she was never the same again. She slowly seemed to lose interest in living. I always knew she felt guilty about my brother's death. I remember she'd once said when she was pregnant with me, she used to lie in her bed every night and pray for a boy, even had my name picked out before she knew for sure I was going to *be* a boy. She'd rub her stomach every night, praying to God to let her son be born healthy. However, by the time she became pregnant with Darryl a year later, she'd found out my father was married to someone else, with a whole other life and separate set of kids. It hurt her so much and made her so angry she no longer wanted his baby. That story haunts me to this day.

In 1993 my mother died from Alzheimer's disease. When she passed away, I asked myself when did my mother's brain stop working, and why? The answer was obvious. It really began ten years earlier, the morning of December 5, 1983, when I was scheduled to speak at the United Nations on apartheid. This was, of course, a great honor for me. I was the first artist invited by the African National Congress to speak to the UN on the subject, an acknowledgment by them that I had turned down four and a half million dollars to appear in South Africa.

Now, here's where it gets a little scary. The day I was set to leave was the same day my mother gave me the devastating news that Darryl had died. What I should have done, I only realized later on, was to have my mother pack her things immediately and come to New York with me. However, I was so shocked at the news of my brother's death, I couldn't think straight.

Meanwhile, the story of Darryl's murder got confused in the press and reports on the radio were saying that *Barry White* was dead. Imagine how I must have felt, riding down the freeway and suddenly hearing my own death announced: *"Barry White died this morning at such and such a place . . . from a gunshot wound to the heart . . ."* I knew my mother heard it, and it couldn't have helped. As I say, I should have taken her with me to New York. Left alone, Mama's mind just couldn't handle the *knowledge* of Darryl's death and began the long process of shutting down from the negative emotional overload. It was for her, and for me having to watch it, a long and excruciating ten-year decline.

After hearing the news, I know I couldn't go through with my speech. I reluctantly bowed out and later sent a letter of apology.

My brother's and mother's deaths were hard reminders to me of why it was never smart to get hung up on false infatuations and other forms of self-adulation (instead of self-love) like stardom. The ultimate definition and reconciliation of one's self is a fiercely private affair and has to come from within. All the fame and money I had in the world couldn't prevent my brother from being murdered or help me save my mother from dying of her broken heart.

I think you can understand why it is I've come to know what is truly valuable in life and what is not. It's something I try never to forget and it's one of the reasons I've always made sure that every day my children know how much I love them.

I'VE BEEN CLOSE to some of the legitimately richest people in the world, as well as those who would like everyone to think they've got it when they haven't. I've met the Sultan of Brunei, a man with wealth be-yond imagination, became good friends with his brother, Geoffrey, and Geoffrey's son Hakim. After them, someone who thinks he has money and tries to impress me with it is going to lose. It's one thing to ride down a billionaire's driveway and pass seventeen Rolls-Royces. It's something else to travel a *two-mile* driveway with seven *hundred* Rolls-Royces and three hundred BMWs, and new sets of each coming in every day. The sul-tan had multilevel glass garages on either side of the driveway, filled as far as my eyes could see with the most extensive private collection of automo-biles in the world.

It appeared that nobody in Brunei who was born there had to work. All the employees came from the Philippines. The people of Brunei were crazy about the sultan. He lived well and made sure his people did too. And, as I say, he knew how to have fun.

I met him when I was invited to perform there at a party in the palace before a private audience of thirty-five people. I'm talking about the entire Barry White Show, including the orchestra and Love Unlimited! We went there, we did it, and we had a ball. The sultan liked it so much he kept inviting us back, year after year, as his personal guests to see whatever show he was hosting. One time Elton John did a performance for about twenty of us.

Just before we'd leave for America, the sultan would ask if there was anyplace else in the world we wanted to see, and he'd include a stop there for me and my people on the return flight.

IN 1975 I HAD a more personal experience that shook me to the core. It began when I ran into my ex-wife, Mary, whom I hadn't seen in the three years since our divorce, and the three kids we were sharing custody of. While she had our children during the week and Glodean and I would get them most weekends, I never actually had to see her.

There is a place called Bill's Taco House on Martin Luther King, Jr., Boulevard. I've been going there for my meat and cheese burritos since I was a teenager. One day I felt like a plate of those delicious burritos and decided to take Blanchard Montgomery, an old friend from the neighborhood, along for the ride. I didn't know it at the time, but taking Blanchard with me may have saved my life as well as Mary's.

Blanchard and I came out of the Taco House and got into my car, and I put my key into the ignition. As I did I happened to look across the street and saw my wife's familiar green Cadillac. She and her new boyfriend had the three kids with them.

Just then the kids got out; I waved to them and they ran to me. As I hugged them, they said, "Daddy, we really miss you," and started crying. I knew our divorce was heavy on them, because when they were babies we were all so tight, and then all of a sudden this man they called Daddy wasn't there anymore.

"I love you kids," I said, and pulled them closer. When I finally let them go, I noticed for the first time their torn and tattered clothes. Here I was paying ten thousand dollars a month to their mother and she was keeping them in what looked to me like *rags*. Meanwhile, I looked over and could see that she and her boyfriend were dressed to the nines. Oh yes, those two looked good! I felt like I was being made into a complete jerk.

That's when I walked back to my car, opened the glove compartment, and reached in for my legal, fully permitted .357. Like every street-savvy musician, I felt the need to be able to take care of myself at all times, especially when I was out by myself. I love people but know all too well there are some crazies out there.

Blanchard grabbed me by the wrist but I was determined. "Let me go, Blanchard."

"I can't let you do it, B.W. . . ."

"I SAID LET ME GO . . ."

Bless his heart, he kept holding on. "B.W., please don't do this. Man, you got so much to live for, and you going to blow it all away on this woman? She's not worth it, B.W."

Those words snapped me out of it. I eased up on the gun, pulled my hand back, and let Blanchard close the glove compartment. Now I got back out of that car and headed once more toward the Cadillac. Mary got out too, and I stared right into her eyes. I didn't say anything. I didn't have to. She knew I meant business. I looked at my kids again, then back at her.

Just then, Nese said, "Daddy, we going to see you again?"

I looked at her and smiled. "You going to see me again. Believe me . . . have I ever made you a promise I didn't keep?"

"Okay, Daddy."

The heat of the moment passed. I went back to my own car, got in, and watched as Mary pulled away.

First thing the next day I saw my regular business affairs lawyer, Larry Thompson. I wanted full custody of my children now, and I didn't care if *I had to pay Mary two hundred fifty thousand dollars to get it!* "I'm sending her all that money," I told him, "and she's dressing them in rags! One way or another she has to be out of their lives."

Larry knew I meant business and promised that a letter would go out to her before the day was out, offering a substantial amount for full custody.

And then something *really* weird happened, the kind of karmic event that has stayed with me the rest of my days. For one reason or another, Monday went by and Larry didn't get around to sending out that letter. Tuesday came, again, no letter. Wednesday, same thing. On Thursday I went back to Larry's office to find out what was going on.

"Barry," he assured me, "I'm sending it today, without fail. She'll get it tomorrow or Monday, whichever way her mail runs."

That sounded good enough for me. The next morning, Friday, I went into the studio and had a great day cutting what would become my next hit single, "I'm Qualified to Satisfy You." At four o'clock I headed home to see the children who were already living with Glodean and me: Shaherah, the baby; Kevin; Bridget; and Barry, Jr., our household of "hers and mine and ours."

Except for Shaherah, they were all fairly close in age and in grade levels at Ridgewood Military School for the boys and Egremont for the girls. I paid a lot of attention to their education and took an active role in their school activities. I made it a point to never miss any academic events. I also made sure we had plenty of play time. After finding out what had happened in school each day, who'd gotten into trouble and who hadn't, I always shot hoops with them on our basketball court. It was a regular family ritual at the "White House," as we liked to call it.

At about six o'clock, I heard a commotion coming from the kitchen. I went to find out what was going on, and that's when I heard my mother, who was visiting us, cry out "Nese!"

It was my thirteen-year-old. She just showed up at my front door, having walked the few blocks from Mary's house, where she'd been living. I could tell she was scared, thinking I was going to be angry that she'd run away from home. "I don't want to live with Mommy," she said through her tears as she put her arms around me. "I want to live with you."

I told Nese to go up to Bridget's bedroom, which she shared whenever she visited, take a shower, and lie down. "But before you do," I said, "bring your clothes down here and put them in the trash." She had some toys with her, and I told her she had to throw those away as well, and I would get her new ones.

The next morning, which was a Saturday, the bell at the front gate rang. I wondered who it could be so early in the morning. I went to the door in my robe and discovered Nina and Darryl. Mary had come by, dropped them off at the foot of the hill, with all their clothes, toys, bikes, everything they owned, and driven off.

I brought them all into the house and immediately called Larry Thompson. "You are not going to believe this, Larry. I've got all my children, man."

"That's great," Larry said. "By the way, I never sent that letter. I'll make proper arrangements to do the right thing and see that everybody's taken care of, legally and *fairly.*"

So I now had all of Glodean's and my kids with us—Shaherah, Kevin, Bridget, Darryl, Barry, Jr., Nese, and Nina. I told the new arrivals the same thing I told Nese: to get cleaned up and put everything they had into the trash. I then asked Glodean if she would take all the children shopping for new clothes and new bikes. From that moment on, I promised myself, their lives were going to change.

I have to say that Glodean was terrific through all of this. She never made any distinction as to who were "her" kids and who were "mine." She treated all of them as if they were one family, and so did I. That's the way we wanted it, and that's the way the kids felt as well. Glodean never showed the slightest difference to any of them, which was so important to their well-being and sense of family.

When they all returned later that day, loaded down with toys and clothes, I told the children that this was going to be a new beginning for all of us, and they were never going to have to worry about where they lived again.

I intended to enroll them in the same schools as the others, according to age. I had their records sent for, and it turned out they were uniformly atrocious. Not only were their grades poor, but they'd been doing a lot of fighting and even a little stealing. I called Mary and asked her about this.

"Barry, they're difficult kids," she said.

I didn't argue with her. "It's cool," I said. "And I'll handle it." It took a lot of time and attention, but eventually they all began to improve their grades and had no more behavioral problems. I made sure they knew how to be polite and nice to people. I taught them what my mother had taught me, that it was nice to be nice. It was important to me to teach this to my children. I was determined to be the spiritual power and moral leader of my family.

This is one of the main reasons I always kept the flow of outside traffic through the house to a minimum. As it was, the kids saw some very heavy people in the entertainment and sports worlds come by, like Michael Jackson, whom by now I'd taken under my wing and served as his unofficial godfather. Jermaine, Tito, and Jackie came by a lot too, as did Muhammad Ali, but I never allowed any informal "hanging out" at my place. My boy Darryl, especially, was a bit too easily impressed by the illusion of fame and celebrity, and I wanted to keep his head on right. I made it my priority to see to it that they understood the reality of the "business" of my life as well as the unreality of the "show."

I also tried to remain friendly with my ex-wife and always reassured her, whenever she asked, that the children were fine. I continued to pay her alimony and was content to leave it at that. Money isn't everything, and in this instance, it was nothing to me compared to the joy of having my children together in a happy household living under one roof.

One of the true joys of parenthood was the deeper appreciation it gave me for my own parents and a more profound understanding of how difficult it must have been for them. That's why I was so happy they both lived long enough to see me succeed. I took care of my mother in every way I could, providing her with whatever she wanted, which wasn't much, and with an abundance of the love that she had instilled in me as a little boy.

Having long ago made my peace with what I knew to be the physical and emotional limitations my father had to deal with in his youth, I wanted to provide as beautiful a twilight for him as I could. Despite whatever anger I may have felt as a boy, when I grew into manhood I felt a great pride to have been born of his seed. One of the things I did was to buy him a brand-spanking new truck. I wanted to buy him a house, but he didn't want it. He said he was happy the way he was. He was his own man to the end. By the time my father passed on in 1982, he had seen me walk into the spotlights of the great stages of the world, and I believe that truly made him a happy man.

NINE

THE SOUND OF DISTINCTION

"LET ME LIVE MY LIFE LOVIN' YOU, BABE"

Now girl you've got my love
You've got my heart and soul . . . forever
The greatest story ever told
How we loved each other

And when the people talk
They will smile and say . . . say
We're the only ones
Who made it all the way . . . hey
Let me live my life loving you

T O T H I S D A Y, *whenever I sing that song, it touches me in a very deep place. My music publisher Abby gave me that title in 1975 while she and her husband, Aaron, were visiting my home in Sherman Oaks. She said she had a title for this new and special piece of music I'd composed, one with deep, deep chord progressions that gave it a wonderfully elegant sound behind its various melodies. I'd first heard it in my head all at once as an explosion of violins and rhythm that came together and evoked for me a beautiful woman and a handsome man making love. I asked what it sounded like to her, and she said out loud, "Let Me Live My Life Loving You."*

I loved that! The song developed into one about a man whose only desire was to love his woman, to take care of her, to share with her, to always be there with and for her. To me that was the real message of the song, because I do indeed want to spend my life loving Lady Music, to continue to write and perform so that I can see the great melody we call life reflected in the eyes of people who hear it. As I said earlier, there are no guarantees in life. Each day I can sit down and write a song, or take to the stage and sing it, is one more day I am indeed fortunate to have.

Perhaps that is one of the reasons it has always fascinated me that the month I wrote "Let Me Live . . . ," I developed polyps on my vocal chords and was told by my doctors I had to change my style of performing or I might not ever be able to sing again. It seemed as if the song had taken on a sacred quality that had to be honored by my never singing it the way I had recorded it.

I couldn't speak at all for thirty days after my operation, and then suddenly, like a miracle, my voice returned, better than ever. I took this as an acknowledgment of the pledge I had made to my muse, a reward for my desire to remain a lifelong devotee, forever faithful to the songs within my heart.

• • •

ONE DAY, IN 1976, I decided to call a meeting at Twentieth Century Records to discuss the plan for promoting my next release and try to get them to put a larger focus on my records. Ever since Larry Nunes's retirement, things hadn't been the same for me at the label. Even with Larry there, we had never been able to crossover Love Unlimited onto the pop charts. I'd just finished a new album, *Let the Music Play*, which I knew could be a mainstream hit, and didn't want to see it overlooked. I decided to meet in person with the head honcho of the whole organization, Dennis Stanfill, chairman of the board of everything at Twentieth, to explain what I thought needed to be done. I sent a telegram off to him.

A month went by without a response. I went to my two managers, Sid and George, and Russ Regan too. We decided to send a second telegram.

Another month went by. Still no answer.

"Boys," I said, "send him *another* telegram. This time tell him I want a million dollars *in cash*, I'll promote the album myself, and I want it delivered in person to me at a meeting in the boardroom."

Russ knew I meant business and decided he'd better go to the board in person to ask for the million dollars. *He got it!* Or at least the promise of it. When Sid told me the news, I said quietly, "Send off *another* telegram. This time say I want two and a half million dollars."

Stanfill wasted no time answering this one. He called me directly on the phone. *"I'm sorry I took so long to get back to you, Barry, but I've been so busy . . ."* And blah blah blah.

What angered me so much was the sheer arrogance. I was, after all, in spite of my inability to break regularly into the white Top 40, the biggest-grossing artist on Twentieth. Between Love Unlimited, the Love Unlimited Orchestra, and me, I was generating about thirty-six million dollars a year for the label. Here I was trying to make them even more money by helping to ensure that my new album crossed over, *and yet I was still a nigger to this white man.* Understand, this wasn't only about money but also respect. It was a war I felt I couldn't afford to lose.

I set a meeting for the Friday before Thanksgiving. That afternoon my team gathered at the house. All my key people were there, among them my chief attorney Larry Thompson, Sid and George, my accountants Eli Boyer and Laurie Fernandez, Russ Regan, and Abby and Aaron Schroeder. Everyone encouraged me to hold my position.

We left together, caravaned over to Twentieth, and went directly to Stanfill's office. Everyone took seats, my team on one side of the room behind me on a couple of leather sofas, the label executives around the table. Then Stanfill entered and said cheerily, to Larry Thompson and *only* Larry Thompson, "Oh, how are you doing?" I took his not acknowledging me as another display of his, and therefore the label's, disrespect.

Fed up and angry, I pulled my .357 Magnum out of the big leather coat I was wearing and without saying a word laid it in front of me on the table. A hush came over the room. Everybody's eyes widened. The already palpable tension suddenly notched up another level. Yes sir, I thought to myself. If you're going to treat me like a nigger, I'm going to put on a real "ghetto gang-banger" show for you.

I began. "Well, Mr. Stanfill, I feel that we needed to have this meeting because there has been a little disrespect here . . ."

"What's the problem?" he said, normally quite eloquent but now sounding a bit scared. "You've got the million dollars. What's the next thing on your agenda?"

"Wait just a minute now, Mr. Stanfill. It's not a million dollars anymore. I thought you knew that. It's two and a half million, *because you've been so disrespectful!*"

With that, he finally went off!

"I'm not going to do it," he said. His face turned red and once again he avoided my eyes. Instead, he went back to Larry Thompson, this time pointing his finger in his face. *"I'm not going to pay two and a half million*

dollars . . . I've already got a million dollars approved by the board, I'm not going back looking like I didn't know what I'm doing!"

"Get your finger out of his face," I said. With that I stood up, grabbed my gun, and shoved it in my pants belt. I then took out a tape of my latest unreleased album, *Let the Music Play*—and did some waving of my own. "You better worry instead about your next record, Mr. Stanfill," I said, and walked out. I was halfway down the studio back lot headed for my car when I heard footsteps coming up behind me.

I turned around and saw Dennis Stanfill running down the permanent New York City outdoor street set waving his arms and shouting after me. *"Come on, Barry . . . come on . . ."* This whole thing was playing out like an action feature. Only this was for real, no camera running, just the real-time clock of my life.

Completely out of breath, he finally caught up with me. "Jesus, Barry, let me talk to you . . . Barry . . . what—what is it . . . you want?"

"I told you. I want two and a half million dollars," I said calmly. "And a new promotion staff to spend it on, so I can make sure my records get the exposure you haven't been able to provide."

He knew if I got into my car it meant the end of my association with Twentieth, which was something we both knew the label couldn't afford. "Wait a minute, wait a minute." He put a hand on my shoulder. "I'll get you everything you want."

We walked back slowly to the building where his office was, through that realistic *Hello Dolly* set of a New York City street, complete with elevated train. Nice touch, I thought to myself, as Stanfill continued to reassure me. "Believe me, Barry, everything is going to be fine . . . You'll have your two and a half million . . . you'll get your promotion staff . . ."

Back in his office, he was a totally different person. "Gentlemen," he announced grandly to the others, "we have come to an agreement. Everything is going to be fine, Barry is going to get two and a half million dollars."

"And I want it by Thanksgiving eve."

"Fine. And," he adds, "I'll have everyone in the press here to see me present you with the check."

I told him not to have anyone there, that my business was my business. Naturally, when I arrived at his office that Wednesday, there were all these reporters, filling up on free food and flowing champagne.

I went into a little private area with Sid Garris. I could always talk frankly with Sid. "You know I don't like flaunting," I told him. "You know how I am. I've never been an asshole. I told Stanfill I didn't want the press here for this."

Sid had the food and drinks removed and apologized to the press. He did keep one magnum of champagne in his office, for a private, ceremonial toast between us. "Let's just have one among ourselves."

Although I didn't drink, I let him pour me a glass. He brought his wife over to meet me, after which I turned to Sid and said, "Shouldn't we all be home with our wives and our children? After all, it *is* Thanksgiving eve." I turned to Stanfill, thanked him for the check, and was out of there.

I was retaught a lesson that day that I'd been learning ever since I first got into the music business. Hassling over money was never *only* about money, but a clear barometer of how a label thinks of artists. The true issue is always respect. Power and control, *then* profit, that's the order of priorities, what those who run the music *business* are really all about. The money they can always make; the power and control is something they have to fight for among themselves, using artists as their pawns.

Let me tell you the real end of this story. In the remaining two and a half years on my contract with Twentieth, the label made every dime of the money they gave me that day *twice over,* on my next two and, for them, final Barry White albums: *Barry White Sings for Someone You Love* and *Barry White—The Man.* Stanfill made his money and so kept his power and control at the studio, while I got a fair measure of what I wanted as well. In business as in love, power yields only to power.

As soon as I walked through my door that night my children greeted me as they always did, with warm hugs and kisses. I took everyone into the living room and showed them the check. "Here it is," I said, waving it around. "I want everyone in this room to know that this money is not just dollars. To me it represents in equal parts my musical talent, self-determination, self-respect, and self-esteem."

I let my kids hold it. Glodean asked if we could take it to her mother's house, so she could see it too. It turned into a wonderful family Thanksgiving celebration, as we had a lot to be thankful for in the White household.

The next day I gave the check to my accountants and asked them to pull a little taste out of it for something I'd always wanted to try—raising horses.

I had my eye on an Appaloosa for a while by the name of Apollo Blue. I told one of my accountants, Eli Boyer, I intended to buy him, and he nearly went crazy.

"No, no, you're not going to get into horses," he cried. "That's how artists always lose everything."

I told him not to worry, that that wasn't going to happen to me because I never planned on racing my horses, which is the big downfall for most breeders. I just wanted to raise them. With great reluctance, Eli laid out twenty thousand for the first, thirty-five thousand for the second, and the same amount for the third.

Now I needed mares.

Back to Eli.

"What do mares cost?"

"Five, ten thousand. Twenty thousand, depending on the bloodline."

Within a year I had 185 horses in Hidden Valley, on property I leased from the great actor Richard Widmark. I loved to drive out there and see them. I used to come around this curve that opened to a view of this magnificent hill filled with my horses. I'd get out and walk among them. Eventually I gave several to my children, so we could all share in this wondrous pleasure.

However, the moment passed when I realized that as much as I loved this hobby, horses weren't my life, music was. Deep down inside, I knew I didn't have the time or the lasting interest to continue with what amounted to a very self-indulgent and expensive hobby. Reluctantly I put feelers out to sell the entire herd, and almost immediately I got an offer

from Mr. Berry Gordy, Jr. He bought every horse I had and fell in love with them just like I had before him.

By the way, I netted over a million dollars in the deal. I guess even well-meaning accountants can be wrong once in a while. And hey, that comes straight from the horse's mouth!

INDEED, BY THE TIME *Barry White Sings for Someone You Love* was released, all my fears about leaving the promotion of the album to the label had come true. By then the entire management and production team, with the sole exception of Russ Regan, had either been forced out or resigned, and apparently the new boys weren't all that impressed with my music. About a month after "Ecstasy," my single off *Barry White Sings . . . ,* my personal homage to the singing and stylings of the great Ray Charles, was in the stores, I received a letter from Twentieth threatening to sue me because it didn't have the "usual Barry White sound." As far as I was concerned, they wouldn't know the sound of an explosion if it went off in the next room. Once again I had turned the lights down and brought the music up, in that now-familiar, idealized haven of romance into which I always took my listeners.

I had put a lot of work into that song and album, and knew the label's attitude was one more salvo in the seemingly never-ending power and control game between Stanfill and me. I decided not to wait them out but to put that money I'd gotten from them to good use. I did my own promotional campaign, went out on the road, and sold the shit out of that album. Sure enough, in spite of all their bitching, it became one of my biggest hits yet. I quickly followed it up with my final album for the label, *Barry White—The Man,* another chart topper. In this one, I wrote about reaffirmation, and meant it as a clear message to Love Unlimited that I was still their Uncle Barry and would be for as long as they wanted. I knew they were hurt and afraid by what had gone down at the label, and I wanted to show them that no matter what, I was behind them. The key song was "I Belong to You," which I knew they would understand. They sang on it, and it, too, shot up the charts, becoming the number one most-played song on every R&B station in the country. Uncle Barry had come through for them again. They giggled when I showed them all the mail I got for them. "Uncle Barry," they said, "you're the baddest! And we're still your babies, right?"

"That's right," I'd tell them. "All three of you. *No matter what.*"

I REMAINED BITTER about the label's actions and knew that having fulfilled my contractual obligations, it was time to leave. Surely I was going out on a record-chart high. The single "Ecstasy" went on to sell more than 3 million copies, as did the album it was from, *Barry White—The Man.*

Still, leaving Twentieth was not an easy decision to make. There were a lot of things I'd loved about being on that label. It was, after all, the one that had put me on top. Nevertheless, in the fall of 1978, I began to shop for a new label. No sooner did word get out than Bruce Lundvall, the president of CBS Records, made a personal call on me at my house to talk things over. "The best deserve to be with the best," he told me. "That's why Barry White should be at CBS."

I took this as a great compliment, because everyone knew Columbia to be *the* premier mainstream label, the class act of popular American music. In spite of that, for reasons of my own, I hesitated. "Bruce," I said, "CBS doesn't need Barry White. I almost went with Clive once, but now I need a label that needs *me,* that will go crazy to make sure my records will jump off those charts. You have five hundred and something other artists who need you more than you need them *or* me."

What I didn't tell Lundvall was that I'd been toying with the idea of starting my own record company. My only problem was financing. It was (and still is today) so much harder for black entertainers at what is essentially the financial investment level in an overwhelmingly white-dominated business. Oh yes, it's fine for black people to make hit records. It's only when we want to keep some of the profits they generate that certain people become very nervous. Even if you're a rap artist or on the cutting edge of hip-hop, when it comes to putting their money where our mouths are, non-black investors remain practically nonexistent.

After virtually no success lining up investors, I reevaluated my position and decided to take Lundvall up on his offer to sign with CBS. I did, however, have two major conditions. The first, I had to have my own label, which I intended to call Unlimited Gold Records. Second, I wanted a reversion deal. This meant the right to release my records in any country CBS didn't and that when my contract ran out, if I didn't choose to stay at the label, ownership of all my master recordings would automatically and permanently revert to me.

This deal raised eyebrows throughout the industry, and I have to credit Abby Schroeder for making it work. It was Abby who kept insisting that if it was going to be my label, then it had to mean I owned what was on it, without qualification.

Of course, Columbia wanted something in return. I agreed not to take any advances for my records. Instead, my money would come strictly from royalties, which would kick in with record sale number one, and a very considerable overhead budget for my label. In short, if my records and label failed I'd wind up having made nothing, but if I succeeded, both the label and I would have made a very profitable deal.

A year later, minus Barry White, Love Unlimited, and the Love Unlimited Orchestra, Twentieth Century got out of the record business. I guess I wasn't so easy to replace after all. What happened was, when I left the label, I took my *sound of distinction* with me, and the implosion created by the loss proved to be too much for company.

I opened up UGR's offices in Studio City. My intention was to develop new acts. I set up an A&R division and was ready to rhumba, baby.

The next two years proved an exciting time for me. Even as I was taking this major  step in my career, I was receiving accolades from some of the most unexpected places. In 1980 the University of Waco, Texas, awarded me an honorary Doctorate of Music for my work with Paul Quinn, a black college.

The following year I received another doctorate in music, this time from UCLA. For a boy who'd never finished high school, who'd received his real education on the streets, this was simply unbelievable. Moreover, this one came from my hometown, which made it especially memorable and meaningful.

NOT THAT I STEPPED directly from a bed of roses into the Rose Bowl, you understand. Two more years of struggling to get my label off the ground took a deep bite out of both my financial and creative banks. By 1984, as the marketplace changed, my string of hit singles slowed and my album sales stagnated. Columbia wasn't interested in any of the acts I had tried to develop, and with the kind of overhead I was carrying I was losing barrels of money.

When it came time to renegotiate my contract, CBS asked me what I wanted, and I told them quite simply I was looking for a way out. Not surprisingly, they didn't seem to mind one bit.

Two weeks later, an elderly messenger showed up at my house to deliver all my master recordings. As he handed them over, he scratched his head and said, "Mr. White, I've been picking up CBS masters all my life. *This is the first time I ever brought them back where I got them from!*"

I laughed, thanked him, put them in my studio, and took a very deep breath. I went to bed that night and slept quite peacefully, believing when I awakened, things would start to get better. They had to, because they surely couldn't get any worse.

Or so I thought.

TEN

LET ME OPEN THE DOOR FOR YOU

"IT'S ECSTASY WHEN YOU LAY DOWN NEXT TO ME"

When we met it wasn't quite clear to me
What you had in store was there only for me.
You took me by surprise,
When I turned and looked I saw the message in your eyes.
There you were, out there on the floor,
The way you moved girl only made me want you more.

I CAN DEFINE *ecstasy in a single word: joy. What a man feels when he lies with a woman he really wants to be with, that's ecstasy. There are many ways to communicate ecstasy. One is to let the spiritual electricity we call love pass from one heart to another. Ecstasy then becomes the medium through which that love passes.*

In the song I am writing about the physical as well as the emotional aspects of ecstasy. I have always held the door open for the ones I love and have always believed there was room at their inn for me. Life is a journey, the stops we make are the romantic outposts that enrich us with true and lasting meaning. When I fall in love with a woman, it is always a total experience, a sexual jolt of pure joy, given as well as received.

Somewhere along the way, we meet and combine to create a oneness, a wholeness that is, for me and I'm sure for you, when experienced with love, the essential life-defining pleasure. "I belong to you" and "You belong to me" are statements that are married to each other. When love becomes the binding yet liberating force, it represents the finest moments of a relationship.

All the rest, I think you'll agree, is what happens in our lives between those moments.

. . .

THE HUGE AND TO MY WAY OF THINKING impersonal CBS system made it impossible for me to continue in the singular vein that had made me so successful in the first place. At the time, the top of their roster was Michael Jackson and Bruce Springsteen. The way they saw it, I was on the wrong side of the profit curve. Just breaking was Luther Vandross, a fantastic artist who could sing, write, and produce his ass off. Not surprisingly, the label was behind him 1,000 percent. I could never get anyone there to work as hard for me as they did for him. I was willing to be in the studio day and night to *make* my albums; I expected the label to do the same to sell them. But they didn't.

I knew I had to somehow return with my music to the independent roots that first brought me into the spotlight and had taken me so far.

After I left CBS, I decided to stop touring. It had been a decision that was a long time coming, as, for the past few years, since 1979, Love Unlimited had decided it was time to go their individual ways. I didn't blame them; in fact, I encouraged the decision. We'd had a great run, and the ladies had had a blast traveling all around the world while building themselves very substantial nest eggs. Now the day had come, as I knew it would, that even though they were sad, because they loved to sing, they were not only ready but eager to get on with the rest of their lives. Linda had found a man she wanted to marry, and Dede returned to school. For the next few years, Glodean and I continued to record together, and for a while I went on the road with her and the orchestra, until, after the debacle at CBS, I realized that for the moment, at least, I too had taken things as far as I could. I needed to make some major changes—to my sound, my surroundings, and to my life. Perhaps the biggest change came in 1988, when Glodean and I decided to separate.

We had come together as friends, which was why we could part the same way. Our time together as lovers, husband and wife had just run its natural course. Neither one of us wanted to pretend something was still there that wasn't, and so we kissed, and said good-bye, and resumed the journey down the paths of our individual lives.

Although our marriage didn't last forever, Glodean and I are still great friends to this day. Our relationship had just evolved to a different place.

It was an example of how things can change, and we both knew it when it did. Because we began as friends it's been easier for us to remain friends, and since we're both into music, we have something we can continue to build on. In that way, my relationship with Glodean will last forever—a beautiful and inspirational thing.

At the same time that Glodean was in some ways moving out of my life—as a lover but not as a friend—another woman, of a very different circumstance, was moving in. When I had first come out of jail, and thought that Mary and I were finished, if you remember I went with another woman. It wasn't anything to do with love, it was really just a sex thing. However, she'd become pregnant, and then Mary did too, and this other woman and I went our own separate ways. At the time no one but the two of us knew we'd had a daughter. She was our secret love child.

Now, some twenty years later, in 1988, while I was on the road, and all these changes were happening in my personal life, I felt I had to correct that situation once and for all. I made up my mind to bring this child into my family. Her name was Denice. I introduced her to Glodean and my children and I must say it was a beautiful thing to see, the way everybody immediately accepted her, as she did them. To this day, we all treat each other as we are, one big family.

Coming when it did, this decision of mine somehow made my separation from Glodean easier, as it seemed to bridge some suspended gap.

I'll always love Glodean, not in spite of who she is, but *because* of it. My philosophy remains the same it's always been when it comes to love, romance, and family. As Billy Joel's great song says, I love you just the way you are. It's not that I didn't understand a woman like Glodean with feelings that were growing and changing. I encourage it, as long as it's for the better, and for herself first.

As for me, I've never changed my feelings about one person—myself. Consistency in my life has and always will be the ultimate rhythm. It's for that reason that everyone knows the same Barry White. After all, if I'm true to myself, who else that matters could ever lie to me?

NOT LONG AFTER MY release from Columbia, I got caught in a major cash-flow squeeze. Even with all my music publishing, a cash-flow lifeline helped keep the wolves from the door. Things got so bad I had to ask my good friends, Wink Martindale, one of the legends of Los Angeles radio, and his wife, Sandy, for a cash loan. He gave it to me without hesitation, no questions asked. That's a friend. His generosity reinfused my creative spirit, and once more I prepared myself to take on the world. Now was the time for me to look back and rediscover what it was in music that had first inspired me, what I had done with that inspiration, and what I still had left in me to do.

WHEN I FIRST HIT big and went on the road, I developed what was, in effect, a three-act variation of a "one-man" show. The Love Unlimited Orchestra would open with twenty-five minutes to set the Barry White feeling in the house. Love Unlimited would follow with another forty-five-minute show—again, all my songs and arrangements. Finally, I'd come out and perform an hour of climactic music. Each act was really a different side of Barry White—the grand, the romantic, and the intimate. My show was a three-tiered reflection of all that I'd seen, learned, and done. I served, then, as the musical host of our collective romance, the messenger of the memories that had spirited our individual lives and loves.

Part of the appeal of my music has always been the same thing I hear

in music that appeals to me. We are all, to a great or lesser extent, natural metronomes. Even people who can't dance can at least tap their feet in time. It is this enormous and universal appeal that we call *rhythm*. I've often gone to clubs when nobody knew I was coming to watch the action from the back of the room. It never failed that when a Barry White record came on, if there had only been ten or fifteen people dancing before, the whole room would get up and start to move. *Rhythm.*

Think about the singers you love the most, and you should recognize that they all have something in common—that *sound of distinction.* In 1965, the first time I heard Levi Stubbs and the Four Tops' version of "Ask the Lonely," I was driving and had to pull over, stop, and crank up the car radio. I couldn't believe it! *The sound of distinction!* Smokey Robinson, Diana Ross, and Michael Jackson have it as well. Marvin Gaye had it big time. Frankie Lymon and the Teenagers, the Coasters, and the Drifters, they all had it.

While I was still a kid, Jackie Wilson came to the Orpheum in downtown L.A. to do eight nights. I became friendly with the security guard at the back door. He got me into every one of those shows for free. What a privilege it was to see this amazing performer work out! He could roll some notes, man, as well as *move* with distinction. There was nobody quite like him onstage. To my way of thinking, all of these performers were truly the Shakespeares of rock and roll.

In the world of pop, there was only one Frank Sinatra. He had the *sound of distinction* for *decades*. When he released his version of "New York, New York," that type of song had really come and gone, but Frank was so great, he was able to reinstate the popularity of an entire genre of music. And did it over and over again, right up until the moment he left us.

In my opinion, the genius of them all was and still is Mr. Ray Charles. To me, he is the number one artist in the world, bar none, the elder statesman of music. He can cry on a record, he can sound humble, or sigh, he can do so much as he sings you his story, and always with style and class. He's like a great actor on a stage performing a magnificent one-man show. He still has more fire, more spirit than anyone else I've ever heard. Go back to his truly amazing renditions of "Georgia on My Mind," "Drowning in My Own Tears," "What'd I Say," and a million more. Man, the cat is *bad*.

Finally, I have to say something for longevity. It definitely has its place: in relationships, in where we live, in the music that we listen to and love. The power of music is such that when you hear a song from ten years ago, if it has *that sound of distinction,* you can remember who you were with, what happened to her, how it went right, if it went wrong and why. Music can pull memories out of years ago like they happened yesterday. Our recorded treasure is truly the soundtrack diary of our lives.

In my music, memories contain the whole package of love feelings—what makes up our emotional *knowledge* of life. I believe the only way the brain eats is through knowledge. Brain food and heart food in the end are the same. The heart food comes from feeling about what you got from it. Because we all know, as much as I sing about it, it's usually either your heart is breaking or my heart is breaking. There isn't anything really happening to your physical heart. We refer to the heart when we mean something sentimental. It's our emotions we're really talking about. When you eat your stomach feels good because it's getting its required nutrition. How do you feed the brain? Through experience that emotionally digests into *knowledge*. That's the only way. And not just love knowledge. Knowledge, period. The more knowledge you have, the better equipped you are as a human being. The more you know, the more you *grow*. As essential as it is for physical food to feed the body, it is no less

essential for learning to feed the mind. It's just as important to have the
nutrients of knowledge supplying your brain as it is to have the nutrients
of food in your stomach. Emotional nutrients are crucial to the accumula-
tion of knowledge.

Spreading the knowledge of love has and always will be the ultimate
goal for me.

WHEN YOU ADD everything up at the end of the day, I think you'd
agree with me that I've been a very fortunate man. What happened to me
happens to very few people in this business. *Forty years and counting,* and
I'm still doing it, as Frank Sinatra said, *my way.*

And still learning. In 1981 my good friend Jack Perry (a Capricorn, of
course), a great musician and producer I'd known since my early, early
days in Hollywood, and who'd worked a little with me on Love Unlimited's first single, "Walkin' in the Rain," came over to help out with some
keyboards for my new album. Talk about small worlds—Jack had grown
up living next door to Glodean!

While he was there, he happened to check on some new equipment
of mine and, by doing so, opened up a whole new world of electronic music. It was Jack who first introduced me to the world of MIDI. In a sentence, MIDI allows you to take a simple melody, feed it into a mixer, and
hear a completely orchestrated version come out the other side. The
introduction of this new way of working helped free me to get more into
myself rather than having to deal with a room full of people. In that sense,
the *electronics* of the technology elevated the *emotions* of my songs, because it allowed me not only to maintain a contemporary sound but to get
further into myself. What many people criticized as the "death" of man-
made music actually helped to bring new life into mine. Similarly, when I
decided to get rid of my regular stable of musicians, everyone predicted it
would be the end of the sound of distinction that had come to define
Barry White. Again, they were wrong. It was really just the beginning of a

whole new era of personal expression, a fresh, contemporary way of using the evolving language of music to say what it was I had to say, in song.

To this day, I do my best work in the studio, most of the time by myself or with Jack. I've been able to refine my music, to the point where just two of us can, and have, made entire Barry White albums, with me singing and each of us playing various instruments and utilizing the latest technology. This has freed me to take the ultimate creative journey, the inner one, to continue to learn *who I am*. To recognize my own creatively spiritual Voice. "Hello. I'm Barry White. Let me open the door for you. The door to experience, knowledge, romance and soul." This is the message I have tried to give to my audience through my music; the same message I've tried to give my children and now to you. *To the best of your ability, know where you are at all times. Know to whom you are talking and what you are doing; and who's talking and doing what to you.*

I'LL TRADE THE ILLUSION of spectacular fame for the reality of everyday kindness any day of the week. When I was first putting myself out on the street, before I became famous or anything, I used to take around these little cassettes, with three or four of my songs on them, to various companies for people hear them. It always amazed me the way certain people would help me, for no other reason than they were good, kind souls. The secretaries, for instance, those crucial, unsung elements in the operation of the machinery of show business, happily extended to me their lovely helping hands. "Barry," they'd say, "why don't you go over to such and such a place, the guy you're looking for will be there at the bar having a drink."

It was that kind of expression of friendship and kindness that made me want to learn how to deal with people, both in the business and in life. I didn't realize it then but everyone who helped me in any way was, collectively, helping me climb out of the ghetto that was my neighborhood and my attitude.

This was not an easy thing for me to accomplish, and it surely didn't happen overnight. All black men come out angry and fighting, because we believe from the get-go that white people own everything—the country, the houses, the major companies. They control not only the money but the *opportunity* to make that money. That's why a black man will say that if a white man can't be successful, it has to be in part because he doesn't want to. But black men and Latinos *start off* angry, because their starting line is already marked twenty feet behind. To me, making it meant getting rid of all that bitterness and anger I was born into, which in turn allowed me to concentrate to an even greater degree on my gift. I learned that when I brought something *positive* to the table, I could turn people on. *All* people.

However, I believe that my success was not just an isolated case of a single man's awakening. There was a harmony to it, a balance that reflected what was happening in this world. Once Mr. Nelson Mandela came to power and helped change the racist policies of South Africa, I changed my attitude toward that country. I now want my music to be heard and sold there, and every one of my albums released in South Africa has gone platinum. I have to say that I am truly *blessed* with the good fortune to be able to take center spot on the world's stage.

In the years I was with Sid Garris and George Grieff, they were always coming to me, saying, "Barry, we should go here, Barry, we should go there." "Oh man," Sid would say, "you're a big hit right now in Brazil, we should go right down there."

"Boys," I'd reply, "don't be in such a hurry to go everywhere." I always believed that if an artist's talent, his gift is real, he doesn't have to use it up all at once.

It was because I felt that way that I didn't do a lot of traveling in the early days of my career. The first place I went to outside of America was England, in 1973, with Love Unlimited and the Love Unlimited Orchestra. I chose that as our first overseas stop because it was the first country where we'd had three number one records there—*and nowhere else.* That is why to this day I never tour Europe without stopping in England: *loyalty.*

The English were my first international fans, and that is something I won't forget.

England was incredible. I'd heard about it my whole life and now was finally getting a chance to see where the great vibrations actually emanated from. It was a super-amazing experience. The girls went crazy, having a ball, like kids in a candy store. They loved bouncing from one country to the next, like different rides at an amusement park. They liked Australia, France, Italy, and so many others. Wherever our music took us, we were willing to go.

Whenever I get on a plane, I like to take a moment and reflect on the great opportunity I have had to see this world firsthand, to visit friends old and new. In 1974 *Billboard* wrote that I'd sold music in countries that didn't even have places where its citizens could buy record players. These are *friends!*

I BELIEVE I'M the only act that has sold out Radio City Music Hall in New York thirteen nights in a row. This happened in 1977, during the two weeks surrounding Valentine's Day. What's great for me is that the feeling I get from fans at Radio City in New York is the same one I get from fans anywhere on the planet. I get a wonderful sense of universality by playing before audiences around the world that somehow makes it seem as if they are the single audience *of* the world.

It wasn't until I began to travel abroad that I fully realized how great America really is and, at the same time, in some ways, how sad. One day I was in Paris having lunch with some friends from the show. We were sitting at an outdoor café, and I noticed these other Americans sitting at the next table, close enough so that I could hear them complaining about everything that Paris didn't have for them. They didn't think the cheeseburger they'd ordered was as good as the cheeseburger they could get in the States. The ketchup wasn't good enough. *And where's the American mustard?* I thought to myself, How backward. Who asked them to go to Paris,

anyway? This was the Parisians' home, not theirs. The arrogance of the guest, this is something I learned a lot more about through the years I spent away from my own home. I also learned about pomposity, self-centeredness, *jealousy.* How anything different has to be inferior. I still wonder how much of a leap it really is from this fellow's attitude toward the natural superiority of "American" cheeseburgers to the ongoing plight of minorities in the United States.

I finally did go to Brazil for the first time in 1982 and *conquered* it! The front pages of the newspapers heralded our arrival. It was the only time in my life I approached the feeling of achieving something like total saturation. It was as if I heard my music and saw myself on TV every minute of the day and night.

Two of the things I love most about Brazilians are their remarkable sense of nationality and how much they like to party. I went to Carnival down there with a video camera and spent twelve hours nonstop shooting the parade. It was truly *amazing!* I was made Grand Marshal for the finale and had the time of my life! Take Carnival away from those people and there will be a revolution in the streets.

I went back to Brazil in 1995 and was deeply gratified to see that I'd actually become *more* popular. My records sold out everywhere and my music was all over the radio. It was an experience I will surely never forget.

Unlike most artists who only play the major cities, I've made it my goal to perform everywhere I possibly can. I've brought my stage show to Italy, Germany, England, France, Switzerland, Japan, Hong Kong, Brunei, Lebanon, Egypt, Africa, and virtually all of Latin America, including Chile, Peru, and Venezuela. A lot of people have seen Barry White and a lot of people have told me they've fallen in love through the beat and message of my music. And I have to believe that it's because the world of love that I write about is a universal one on the minds and in the hearts of all people everywhere, since the beginning of time.

ANYWAY, THERE I WAS, in 1986, ready, willing, and able to take back the reins of control on my own storied career. One of the first things I decided to do was revisit a man I'd first discovered in 1982, a fellow from India by the name of Chakroponti who, as it happened, was the official astrologist for the prime minister of India.

I first went to see him to have my chart done. He said it revealed all my talents, my gifts, my penchant for being a realist. And then he told me some things that absolutely sent *chills* through my body, like for instance why my dad was never there for me as a child. "Your father," he said, "was forbidden to have anything to do with raising you. Only a woman with the right knowledge could have made you into the person that you are."

He also said, "One day toward the end of next year you're going to lose somebody you love very much, but it will pass. You will handle it the way you've handled everything else in your life." At the time I thought he was talking about my mother. For the next year I was taking extra lookouts for Mama, and as December drew to a close, I began to doubt Chakroponti. Then, on December 5, 1983, my brother was shot in the heart and killed.

Chakroponti's awareness of the astrological motion of our lives affects me deeply. The more I get into it, the more I realize how important, how *crucial* it is in our understanding of one another. Once I know someone's sign, I begin to know what to look for in him or her as a human being. I still have to get to know the person, but at least I have a pathway to follow to that knowledge.

Every sign has its weaknesses and its strengths. They help you know what field you're playing in. Some have luxury seating. Others are clearly marked KEEP OUT. Take Aries, for instance. They're always good business-people, meticulous about work. That's always the first thing I think of when I meet an Aries. Diana Ross is an Aries. Marvin Gaye was as well. The more you know, the more you grow, and the astrological charts are an excellent way to get to know yourself better. Most people don't want to know their whole story, but my philosophy is just the opposite, that what you don't know *will* kill you.

Astrology has helped me understand that I'm a servant by nature. I want to allow people to pass through my hallway of knowledge and experience, whether for the sake of their career or in pursuit of the one they love. When I'm in concert I tell the audience I'm their servant that night. My style is to serve up musical and spiritual knowledge hot, fast, and with a lot of excitement.

But in the end, I'm not merely an "entertainer." Don't come to a show only looking for entertainment. I'm not going to bring you just that. I'll say what you want me to say, sing whatever you want me to sing, and hope that my wisdom and philosophy get through as well. I always try to remain philosophical about the business of creative expression. I have always pursued my gifts in an honorable way; therefore, I can hold my head high.

IN 1986, shortly after I visited Chakroponti, Jesus Garber, my old and dear friend from the early promotion wars at Twentieth Century, came to me and said, "I think I can get you a deal at A&M."

As you may imagine, having left CBS, this was an enormously appealing proposition to me. A&M, the brainchild of Herb Albert—"A"—and

Jerry Moss—"M"—began in Herb's garage and was the hot new "kid" on the block, the latest in the great tradition of independent rock and roll labels.

Of course, I told Jesus I was interested. He set up a meeting with John McClain, the head of A&R at the time (he would go on to become one of the pioneers of rap), and who was determined to expand the label's then very white, as in the Carpenters, roster into the realm of contemporary R&B. We got together in a Hollywood restaurant, and by the time lunch was over, we had made the deal. *I was back in the big show!*

I knew I was someplace special the first time I planted my feet on A&M's famous Hollywood studio lot, originally built by Charlie Chaplin to make motion pictures. This was the locale of the legendary sound stage where so many great recordings and videos had been made, including the famous *We Are the World* album and video. I could sense Chaplin's strong karma everywhere on the lot and felt an affinity with the man. Like me, he was an independent-minded artist whose work found its fullest expression when he was free to make it exactly the way he wanted. He was a people's artist, as I am, and a man whose work I have always responded to on a visceral level.

It was just around this time I ran into my old friend and attorney Ned Shankman, who'd handled my divorce from Mary and whose firm I'd been with until Larry Thompson had gone his own way. The occasion was a 1987 BMI luncheon honoring me as one of the newest members of the "Million Airs Club," a recognition of songs that have achieved the million-airplay mark on radio. The song was "Love's Theme." (In 1999 it passed the 3 million mark.)

Ned and I, meanwhile, exchanged phone numbers, and a few days later he got in touch with me. He came to my house to get caught up. I had let Sid and George go in 1975 and used the services of Larry Thompson, Ned's partner in the law firm, until Larry decided to go into the film business. Ned then offered to look over my finances and realized I needed to straighten things out, and fast.

The first thing that had to happen was the release of a new album. Unfortunately, for a while it looked as if I were in danger of running headlong into the same kind of chaos I'd just come out of. No sooner had I begun work on the album than Jerry Moss and Herb Albert sold their label to Polygram, one of the largest record conglomerates in the business. So there I was, back in the same old corporate shit storm.

I tried to keep this from upsetting my focus and to concentrate all my efforts on making my album, but everything seemed different. For one thing, I wasn't quite as hot as I'd been in the past. Rap and hip-hop were coming on strong. There's a whole new generation out there, and a whole new sound.

I also wanted to regroup Love Unlimited and the Love Unlimited Orchestra. Unfortunately, there were unexpected obstacles.

Without question the worst was the untimely death of Dede, who'd come down with cancer and passed away at the sweet and tender age of only thirty-nine. She was still a baby when she passed away in my house, where, once she got sick, I insisted she stay until the end came. It was incredibly difficult to watch her waste away to nothing.

Her unfortunate passing changed forever the chemistry of the group. Not long after, Linda married a doctor she'd fallen in love with, and they decided to live full time in Switzerland, where she went on to become a certified nurse, working alongside her husband.

Glodean, then, became the only remaining original member of Love Unlimited. I was delighted when she said she was so happy I was reforming the group. Although we still toured together, the last time we'd actually worked together in a studio was in 1981, when we recorded an album of duets that I produced called *Barry and Glodean.*

I added two of my daughters, Shaherah and Bridget, to the new mix, and decided to call the group Love U II. As in *Love to what? Love to Love You, Baby!* And we were off and running once more!

When I finally did finish *The Right Night and Barry White,* Ned decided it would be a good idea to launch the album with a grand tour of Europe. I agreed, but insisted on maintaining the integrity of what people had come to expect from a Barry White concert. I wanted a full thirty-two-piece orchestra, the organized Love U II, all of it. In the end, I may not have made as much money on this tour as I could have but I met my true goal when I found myself back on a big stage performing before sold-out international audiences.

Everywhere in the world we played I was treated like a conquering hero. We did fabulous shows in Monte Carlo, performed on New Year's Eve in Paris, a show that knocked me out because it was mobbed by young people wanting to see me do my *thang*. I believe that show marked a turning point in my so-called comeback, although as far as I was concerned, the continuing airplay my music had gotten from day one meant I'd never really been away at all.

From that night on, everywhere we went we sold out every seat in the house. The buzz became so loud A&M heard it all the way back in the States, and decided to put the kind of push behind me usually reserved for their biggest and most happening stars.

Happily, I found my audience in America was still there when they put me right back onto the charts.

IN 1994 I WROTE and produced a new Barry White album, *Put Me in Your Mix*. Both the album and single broke big, and once more the voice of Barry White seemed everywhere. *"Put me in your mix, Whatever your mix is. That's called cookin'."* I was talking to my fans from the heart, and they knew it.

I also started doing bigger and better shows, incorporating the history of my music as a sort of backdrop to the grandeur and splendor of peace. I went to landmark places, like Egypt, and literally turned my concert into a showcase for international harmony and unity. This feeling culminated in my 1995 album, *The Icon Is Love*. I especially love this particular album, a culmination of everything that preceded it. This one has a sense of history embodied within the textures of my music, like the finest aged wine or the longest and most loving of relationships.

The Icon Is Love!

I was in the middle of an eighteen-month-long world tour to promote the album when something happened during an unanticipated two-week break in October 1995 that almost put the lights out on me for good. I had been suffering for a long time, without knowing it, from hypertension, one of the deadliest and most insidious of afflictions. I'd been unusually tired for most of the tour, falling asleep early in the night, sometimes on the bus on the way back from the concert to my hotel room. For the first time in my life I had to cancel shows, because I just didn't have the energy to go on. It finally found a way to show itself, by attacking my kidneys and putting me face to face with death. Surely, I thought, this was the end.

I'd faced death before, back in my gang-banging days when I didn't have much to lose. Now, here I was, with *everything* on the line, about to lose it all.

I was in Las Vegas on Halloween eve when suddenly I felt this horrible, awful pain in my stomach. Now, understand, I'd never really been sick a day in my life. I guess I'd saved it all up for this one big attack. One minute I was fine, walking around the house, the next I was kind of delirious. I sat down on my bed and couldn't get my head together. Before I knew it, I was in a hospital, unconscious, fighting for my life. For four days I lay in an open-eyed coma, with my close friend Jack Perry by my side, holding my hand, holding me here, trying to keep me from slipping out of this world. I remember trying to pull Jack along with me, into the vast unknown that kept calling, and his hand, like the other side of a tug-of-war, fighting to keep me on the side of the living.

Jack, my son Kevin, and my daughter Nese were all there three days later when I opened my eyes. I could tell from the look on their faces I'd pulled through, and that they were grateful for my survival and amazed at the same time. It was one of those so-called miracle cures, because the doctors didn't have a clue as to how to bring me back. I'd been a fighter all my life. Now I'd been in the championship bout, and while on the ropes in the fifteenth round, I scored the biggest KO of my life!

As soon as I was well enough, I went back on the road, the chance to once more entertain my fans having taken on a new and far more profound meaning for me.

· · ·

WHEN THE *ICON* TOUR ENDED, I started doing commercials, which I'd never thought much about before. I'd always been reluctant to lend my prestige to endorsements. However, the quality of the products was so high and the offers so strong that I went for it. I'm not saying I was the first by any means, but before me there were relatively few rock stars doing it *for themselves,* and an even smaller percentage were black. Before the decade ended, everyone from B.B. King to Aretha Franklin was getting a chance to be heard anew, to lend their voices and songs to commercials. I'd like to think that I added some measure of validation to the practice when I helped break down that particular wall and discovered a new way to sustain the income of other performers, feed their families, and pay their bills.

My first voice-over was for McDonald's. It proved one of the most successful endorsements of all time. The popularity of the famous chain escalated noticeably, due at least in part to an ad a lot of people still remember. The comedienne Sandra Bernhard recently quipped that she had been a lifelong vegetarian until she heard Barry White's voice on that commercial.

I followed this with several endorsements for Chrysler's Jeep Grand Cherokee, and that vehicle became the best-selling SUV in the world. I'm not saying it happened because of me, but I don't think having my voice hurt them any! AT&T has since come aboard, Arby's, Kraft Foods, and so many more. Eventually, to handle all the offers, I started my own company, Unlimited Jingle Factory. The only thing I get asked to do more than commercials are phone-answering machine messages, and I may just start a separate branch of the company for those!

I guess TV and I agree with each other. I allowed a character on *The Simpsons* TV show to be modeled after me and supplied the voice. This happened in 1989, and I'm still amazed by the incredible reach of that show. I was recently on tour in Australia, where I hadn't been in years, and at least in part because *The Simpsons* airs there, I was greeted with sold-out crowds everywhere I went. I held a press conference where one female reporter kept asking me all these detailed questions. She happened to be Japanese. I asked her age and was surprised to learn she was only nineteen. I couldn't resist asking her why she was so interested in Barry White, and she said she became a fan of mine because of *The Simpsons!*

THE INFAMOUS 1994 NORTHRIDGE earthquake accomplished what nothing and nobody had been able to do before: It drove me out of Los Angeles. Of course, I'd lived through many earthquakes in L.A. before that one. They usually rolled in a certain way, created a kind of swaying action.

Not this time.

It felt like somebody had literally picked up my house and slammed it down hard into the concrete. The sensation was something like standing in the center of a series of bomb blasts.

It struck after I'd spent a long night working in the home studio I built on the hill above the big house in Sherman Oaks. It was about four in the morning. I walked into my bathroom, brushed my teeth, went to the bedroom, and sat down on the side of my bed to do a little planning for the next day when all of a sudden I heard a low, groaning *whoomp!* I glanced around as I felt a jolt that rattled the entire house from the ceiling down to the basement. I rushed through my door to get outside and saw what looked like a tidal wave pouring out of my pool. The waterfall was completely destroyed.

The entire main house was moved off its concrete foundation. It was a miracle, one I am eternally grateful for, that none of us was hurt.

When the sun came up I could see the extent of the damage all along Ventura Boulevard. It looked like wartime. A month later I closed on a house in Las Vegas and was out of there.

As it turned out, I wasn't that crazy about living in the desert. My main objection to Vegas came in my fourth and what turned out to be my final year there—the extreme shift in the weather. Except for a brief span of about three weeks, the temperature is either very hot or very cold. I concentrated my efforts on finding a new, more permanent home.

After doing some careful research, I came to the conclusion that San Diego was the safest place in the state in which I was born and wished to continue living. There had never been a huge disaster there, the weather was always beautiful. And I found a house right by the water, which is how I like to live. I hate being landlocked. Maybe it was because I was brought up in the prison of the ghetto streets and have always felt the need for a sure way out, a permanent escape route. Whatever the reasons, I found the perfect sanctuary from where I regrouped yet again, ready to come out with another new album, and a renewed connection to my great audience of fans the world over.

My fall 1999 album, *Staying Power,* is all about just that—the many levels of staying power that have proven to be the definition of Barry White. There's the sexual element, of course, here used as a romantic metaphor, meaning the longevity of physical *and* emotional love, and there is the professional meaning. I think after forty years in this business I can safely say that I do indeed have staying power!

Puff Daddy did some work on the album. He's an enthusiastic young man who shows a lot of merit in what he does. He really came through for me. Jack and I sent him a tape of a remake of Sly Stone's "Thank You," and I told him what we wanted. We love what Puffy did and added a few things

of our own. I first met him in 1995, while I was on tour behind *The Icon Is Love.* He seemed to be a nice guy, quiet, humble, respectful, polite, and loaded with talent. He let it be known that he'd give anything to work with me. I told him if the opportunity ever came, I'd certainly

give it to him. I don't make promises I can't or won't keep, and when the time was right, we called on him and he responded.

Chaka Khan and Lisa Stansfield join me on a song as well, "The Longer We Make Love (the Closer I Get to You)," written by my dear friend Aaron Schroeder, and Marlin Saunders. There's some wonderful sounds on this one.

I'M THRILLED THAT Glodean and I are still making music together. She's on the new album, and sounds as good as ever, if not better.

I've been truly fortunate in my career to have enjoyed such a long run. With the new album, I want to bring everyone to yet another place in my life and theirs. I'm as excited about being in the studio today as I was the first time I ever walked into one. I've survived, and so has my music. It is the constant, ongoing journal of my life and the lives of those I've known and loved. In so many ways we've experienced staying power together. This isn't an album I could have made when I was twenty. It is a reflection of my staying power, which wouldn't have been possible without yours for me, and for that I have to say thank you from the very bottom of my heart and my soul.

ELEVEN

DESIRE AND ABILITY

"STAYING POWER"

Lady I've made plans
In a fancy restaurant where we can dance
Put on my favorite dress
You know the one that oozes sexiness

*S*O *HERE WE ARE, in the ballroom of the ongoing dance of life. My date for the evening is my favorite lady, Ms. Music. No matter what happens, we'll always have each other. Our love songs can represent many things, but few things can represent love songs. As long as we continue to hear the music, we are alive, and as long as we are alive, we can love.*

In my music, there have been three major "acts" of my life presented in album form. The first set was about falling in love. The second was about being in love. The third is about staying power—the importance of the ability and commitment to keep it together in love, in life, in career, in the hearts and minds of people who love music. There may be obstacles, there may be bad times, but please, ladies, and you men too, let yourself open to the love and the warmth and the magic that music will bring. If you do, your life will be so much more enriched, enlivened, and exciting. During my hardest times, I have always looked to the good Lady Music, and she has never let me down.

Because I've dedicated my life to her, she has smiled on me. She doesn't smile on everybody. Sometimes she smiles on someone only once or maybe twice. In the year 2000, I will be celebrating my fortieth year in this business.

• • •

THE SUN IS BEGINNING to sink a little lower into the ocean. I sit back and breathe in the warm San Diego air. I have indeed come a long way, although my journey is surely nowhere near its end. Rather than thinking my best years are behind me, I prefer to believe, as the song says, *the best is yet to come!*

So many extraordinary things, so many privileged moments, so many powerful changes, so many ups and downs. Through it all, I still love music, still love to listen to it, to make it, to perform it, to *live* it.

In 1975 *Billboard* magazine gave me its Disco Forum Award for being "The Man Who Started It All." While I always appreciate accolades, the truth is my music was never, strictly speaking, "disco." I simply liked to make music to dance to and make love by, and as far as I can see it doesn't matter if you're in a disco, a house, a club, at the beach, or in a park.

In the end, disco is just another step in the great cultural dance we call popular music. Be it ballroom, swing, R&B, it all comes from somewhere and, if it's popular enough, assimilates the cultural roots that produced it into the mainstream. American disco in the 1970s came out of Europe; that's where people went to hear this new *black* music no one wanted to play in white clubs. You wanted to hear

black music, you went to discos. Once it became popular, Americans ate it up, and me along with it, in that great 1970s pop cultural tidal wave.

Lisa Stansfield's 1990 "All Around the World," the number one dance record that year, sounds a lot like one of my songs, and a lot of people think I wrote it, but I didn't. It's actually the very talented Ms. Stansfield emulating my style, which is always, to my way of thinking, one of the great compliments in the world. She followed it up by actually recording one of my songs, "Never Gonna Give You Up," which brought it back to the charts for the *second* time.

I have to appreciate when another artist acknowledges my music. I am told that I am one of the most sampled artists in the world. Apparently, a lot of the young rappers hear something in my music that makes them want to attach a piece of it to their own.

OVER THE LAST THIRTY YEARS, I managed to become a huge crossover act, in more ways than one. White men and women, for sure, as well as gay men and women, fell in love with Barry White. I have always appreciated my gay fans. I have Latin fans, black fans, Japanese, French, Brazilian, and Italian fans. Make no mistake about that, I *really* have Italian fans. In 1976 at Westchester's Premiere Theater, one of the "families" came to my concert. They brought grandmothers, grandfathers, children, wives, everybody. After the show they all came back and crowded into my dressing room. One big guy grabbed my cheek and said, with conviction, "Barry, if you ever need anything, you just call us."

DJs often refer to me as the original rapper. Again, while I feel complimented, the truth is, it's really not my thing. I've never "rapped" on a record. Rap, though, is cool, and will always be with us, as will hip-hop, because there are new ears out there, and the subtle shift in approach from people like TLC, what they have to say and the way they say it, is what keeps music so alive and vital.

People seem to want to hear me through the rhythms of whatever style of music is popular. I've recorded very few songs by other writers, preferring to write and perform what is an extension of my own creative expression. I did have a hit with what I consider one of the best love songs ever written, one that is probably closer to a Barry White tune than any other—Billy Joel's classic pop tune "Just the Way You Are." Billy caught a moment, and he remains to this day gracious and generous in his praise for my version, even when so many people think that because I had such a hit with the song I must have written it. The day he told me he loved my recording of his tune I felt deeply complimented by one of the world's great songwriters.

"Standing in the Shadows of Love," recorded by the Four Tops, written and produced by Holland, Dozier, and Holland, remains my favorite of the songs I've recorded by a writer other than myself. The shadow is the supreme place to observe the game of love while being in it. The darkest place to run, where there still is just nowhere to go. Why? Because it is the shadow of *doubt*.

In Belgium one time the Four Tops and I happened to be on the same show. Levi Stubbs told me opening night how much the Tops loved my version of "Shadows." That made me feel so proud. He'd only heard it on record, because I've never sung it live. I'm planning a return trip to Egypt one day, this time to perform live in front of those great monuments in the desert. I'm going to open with that song, *standing in the shadows of the great pyramids!*

I've also recorded my version of the incredible Jesse Belvin's "Goodnight My Love and Beware." Although Jesse was much older than I was, we did grow up in the same neighborhood—one of the reasons I suppose I've always felt a special affinity for him, as well as a love for his style of singing. I even went to his services at Angeles Funeral Home on Jefferson when I was seventeen, after he was killed in an awful car crash. "Goodnight My Love and Beware" is a song from the 1950s that remains truly timeless. It was one of the first songs I ever put together with an image of the person who recorded it. It made me aware of the name of the singer as well as that of the song. By doing so, it opened up a new layer of what this phenomenon called music was really all about.

One of the strangest and most delightful recordings I've ever heard is this funk thing laid down by Fun Lovin' Criminals they call "Love Unlimited"—they sing, "If Barry White saved your life, . . ." A great sound, a very funky beat. I love it to death. Thank you, boys.

In my opinion, the greatest love song of all time is the Flamingos' recording of "I Only Have Eyes for You." The first time I heard that song, coming home from school one day in 1959, I was with a bunch of other students, and to this day I've never seen the reaction in women to a song the way I did then. That song did more for us boys trying to get next to our girlfriends than anything else we tried! It also taught me a lesson I've never forgotten. So *that's* how women react to a musical sound they really like. *How pretty it is . . . how soft it is . . .* These are things I've tried to take with me into the studio each and every time I've gone in, to lay it down on my tracks, so that they come out as pure as possible on the other side of the stereo.

There are two times in my life when I'm happiest—loving someone and making a record. Usually, these two go together. Both are expressions of my true, inner feelings.

Right now I have the feeling on both sides. I've just finished recording

a new album, and the woman I love, Katherine, is one of the sweetest I've ever had the privilege to know. Among her best qualities is that she's without games and always willing to listen and learn. Often we stay up until four o'clock in the morning, talking about nothing, anything, and everything. I've found that a good relationship is all about sharing your *mind* as well as your *time* with another human being. True inspiration comes when I can teach my lover something and she can teach me. That is the glory of the human side of life. Otherwise it's just passing in the night avoiding icebergs. I've said I'll never get married again, but in truth, those are just words. I'm *with* Katherine, and she's *with* me, and that's what counts. We each know there are no guarantees. We just love each other and will let time take care of itself.

Because of all the things that are continuing to come to me in my life, I'm as happy as I can be. I'm busier than ever. In recording, we're negotiating for a movie. There's a millennium world tour happening. There's talk of making a movie about my life. Several of my songs have been used on the popular *Ally McBeal* television program, including "Love Serenade," which always introduces one of the characters. Last season they actually wrote an episode for me to appear in which I sing "You're the First, the Last, My Everything." The audience for the taping cheered wildly, which I so appreciated. The scene took place in a nightclub, at Case's birthday party. After dancing to my music alone for inspiration throughout the season, for his birthday the other lawyers in his office decided to throw a party for him at a club where I appeared and sang his favorite, "Everything." This was a special moment for all of us.

I recently filled Madison Square Garden in New York City for a benefit, and many contemporary R&B stations have a lot of Barry White music on their playlist. New York's Kiss-FM, which in 1998 inducted me into its Artists' Hall of Fame, has thirty-two songs of mine in its current rotation!

I've done every TV talk show, from Arsenio to Jay Leno to the great Oprah Winfrey. I've also done David Letterman several times, which I continue to hear about from my fans. I'd already done his show once when he asked me back to appear on his 1997 prime-time anniversary show. All he wanted me to do was say a few isolated words and names—"Pataki" and "fat ass ham"—that he told me wouldn't mean anything if someone else said them, but when Barry White did, look out! After that, for the longest time, everywhere I went, all I heard was "Barry, the way you said 'fat ass ham' and 'Pataki' was the funniest thing . . ."

I'm set to celebrate the first rhythms of the next millennium by giving a New Year's Eve show in Belgium the night the old century ends and the next thousand years begin.

After I finish adding up all of the wealth, fame, and notoriety, I look at what I have gotten out of music that is truly *valuable.* From 1960 when I first tried to make music for a living through today, right now, I *did something with my life!* When my career finally does come to an end, I will have the privilege of the greatest memories to look back on and relive. Songs I love and remember so well, people who have come in and out of my life, moments I have shared with lovers, friends, and family.

I've learned the value of being myself, to be the best *me* that I can be, to do my thing, to create my sound, to perform my own magic, to communicate my own feelings. I only and always wanted to be the best Barry White.

Be yourself. That's lesson number one, two, three, and four thousand.

FROM THE BEGINNING, I never expected anything. I just wanted to make music. I had no idea this desire would so profoundly define my life and give me everything I ever dreamed of and beyond. If I hadn't gone into music, I might have stayed in the toy business, because of how much joy it gave me to see the faces of those little children light up every day. How different my life might have been if one or two things had turned out other than they have!

How fortunate I truly am that I clicked with the public and was allowed the grace of time to continue to develop and refine my sound, so as to be able to work it up for the long run.

In that sense, performing has always been a mystical thing for me, regal and majestic. When I walk out on that stage and sometimes get out no more than "Good evening ladies and . . ." *Bang!* I hear that audience's roar that comes from the back, front, and sides of wherever I am and then explodes toward the stage. It's a mammoth, collective greeting from my fans, their way of saying "Glad to see you, Barry!"

It's one of the things that makes the rougher aspects of touring—the packing, the flying, the unpacking, the hotel rooms, the hours, the jet lag, the bad food—all of it worth its weight in gold. On balance, I might rather be at home working on a new song, figuring out an arrangement, playing with the board until the sound is exactly the way I want it. The difference is, in the studio, the world belongs to Barry White. On stage, Barry White belongs to the world.

And because of that I promise I will keep on putting it out there for you, as long as you want it. Your gift to me is a reflection of mine to you, and there is nothing else quite like that exchange of love that I've ever known. I thank you so much for allowing me to have shared my music, my memories, and my love with you.

So now, as the night comes upon us, why don't you sit back, relax, and, one more time, my friend, let me turn you on. Let me take over. I'll be happy to do all the work. Together we can work miracles. And always remember, remember, we are playing in the kingdom of the gods—*I am, you are, and it is.*

As our journey continues.

ACKNOWLEDGMENTS

Barry White

For many years, people have wanted me to write the story of my life. For whatever reasons, I never wanted to do it before. The time wasn't right, events were happening too quickly, my world was evolving at too fast a pace for me to want to stop and reflect. Now, as the century comes to an end, it seems right to me to *begin* to reflect on the first part of my life.

I've been very honored to take this biographical adventure with my good friend Marc Eliot. He's really taught me a lot. I believe you never stop learning. That's why as long as I'm living I keep on the alert. Doing this book has been very comfortable for me. I've never felt the strain or frustration other people may have when faced with putting the story of their lives down on paper. I guess it's because my story was ready to be told, and I had a terrific partner to help me do just that. The experience can be summed up in a single word. *Extraordinary.* Thank you, Marc, for sharing your knowledge with me.

Of course, on a whole other level, I must thank my mother and father, for without them I wouldn't be here. My mother gave me the most wonderful guidance imaginable. My father didn't have a lot of input in my life, but I didn't really need a father. What I needed was a wise woman, and in my mother, I was blessed to have one.

I also want to thank Larry Nunes, who in many ways was like a real father to me. To this day, outside of my children, I haven't met anyone I love, admire, and respect more than I did Larry. I owe my career to him.

My children come next. They were the motivation for me to get serious, to try to make a life in music, to be able to support them. They helped me straighten out my life and keep me on the right road. I thank them more than they could possibly know and love them without limits or exceptions. I thank my wives, the ones I've had and the one I will have. Each brought a new knowledge to me, and I am grateful to them all. I also want to thank each and every one of my wonderful grandchildren. They are Tyerré, Tyronne, Tamara, Sheneta, George, Myisha, Sharnea, Brittany, Justine, Dominique, and Ayannah Love Settle. I love you all.

How do you thank people like Aaron and Abby Schroeder, who have so beautifully watched over my career and my life for the past thirty-one years? These are not business associates, these are family members as far as I'm concerned.

I thank the judge who sent me to jail when he did, because he helped me understand that that wasn't the life I wanted. I'd also like to thank two teachers I had whom I told you about in my story: Mr. McCombs, my homeroom teacher, whose distinct character I loved, and Miss Everson, who was quite a lady. Both of these teachers were very, very important to me in ways they probably never knew. They helped set me straight, onto the right path.

I also want to thank Larry Thompson and Ned Shankman for all they did for me. Also J.P.—Jack Perry, my conductor and my soul brother. We've been together twenty years, every day. The joy I get out of being around and with Jack, our friendship is so strong, it's scary. He's a Capricorn, just like Larry was. In so many ways, Jack for me is a continuation of the spirit of Larry Nunes.

And of course, my fans, the people who have taken the time to make my music part of their listening pleasure. I can never fully express how thankful I am to you. My fans have given me everything I have, and made me everything I am.

Marc Eliot

It is always a privilege to be in the presence of a legend. Working with Barry White has been a nonstop joy for me. I've loved his music from the first time I heard it on the radio, danced to it and other things, and now, having gotten to know the man, appreciate it and him on a much more personal and meaningful level.

When Barry and I first got together to discuss the possibility of this book, there were far more obvious differences between us than any place of common ground. Barry is black, raised in the ghettos of South Central L.A., and a man with a large and loving family. I am white, from New York, have no family, and am very much the loner. Yet, from the moment we met, there were special and strong bonds between us. We both shared a lifelong admiration for Malcolm X. Barry has a beautiful portrait of the man above his fireplace that became our first common touchstone. Barry had met him as a child; I had the privilege at a rally at Columbia University. Each of us had a brother who'd died too young and too violently, and both bear the permanent scar of our respective losses. Each of us pulled our way up by our bootstraps from the mean and vicious streets with the desire to make something out of our lives, and each has done so in an honorable fashion. In order to tell a good story, which I hope we've done, you have to have one, which Barry White definitely does. The time seemed right for us to put our heads together and tell this one the way we did.

However, what really sealed it for us was one afternoon early on when we sat in Barry's living room listening to the world's greatest stereo play just about the entire Motown catalog. We sang along, we pointed out our favorite parts, we conducted the orchestra, we bounced to the beat. We laughed, we cried, we *connected*. It is a day I shall never forget. Thank you, Barry White, for the opportunity of letting me get to know you and for the privilege of listening to so much great music with you on so many wonderful occasions, the opportunity to pass endless hours talking knowledge, and for the truly delightful experience of working together. How proud I am indeed to share this byline with you, my friend.

I also wish to thank the following people: Ned Shankman, Kevin

White, Jack Perry, Aaron and Abby Schroeder, Katherine Denton, and Mary Romeu. These are Barry's people, and each has been extremely helpful, warm, and embracing.

On my end there is Mel Berger, my longtime friend and agent; Chi-Li Wong, whose love, devotion, and support were crucial; Lauren Marino for her faith and patience; her assistant, Ann Campbell; and as always, the chairman of my board, Dennis Klein.

BARRY WHITE
DISCOGRAPHY

ALBUM	RELEASE DATE
20th Century Records	
1. I've Got So Much to Give	1973
2. Stone Gon'	1973
3. Can't Get Enough	1974
4. Just Another Way to Say, I Love You	1975
5. Barry White's Greatest Hits, Volume I	1975
6. Let the Music Play	1976
7. Is This Watcha Wont?	1976
8. Barry White Sings for Someone You Love	1977
9. Barry White—The Man	1978
10. I Love to Sing the Songs I Sing	1979
11. Barry White's Greatest Hits, Volume II	1980
Unlimited Gold Records, Inc.	
12. The Message Is Love	1979
13. The Best of Love	1980
14. Barry White's Sheet Music	1980
15. Barry & Glodean	1981
16. Beware!	1981
17. Change	1982
18. Dedicated	1983
A&M Records, Inc.	
19. The Right Night & Barry White	1987
20. The Man Is Back!	1989

BARRY WHITE
I've Got So Much to Give
(1973)

Produced by: Barry White
20th CENTURY RECORDS, a subsidiary of 20th Century Fox Film Corporation

SIDE ONE

Standing in the Shadows of Love
Holland/Dozier/Holland

Bring Back My Yesterday
Barry White/Robert Relf

SIDE TWO

I've Found Someone
Barry White

I've Got So Much to Give
Barry White

I'm Gonna Love You Just a Little
More, Baby
Barry White

BARRY WHITE
Stone Gon'
(1973)

Produced by: Barry White
20th CENTURY RECORDS, a subsidiary of 20th Century Fox Film Corporation

SIDE ONE
Girl It's True, Yes I'll Always Love You
  Barry White

Honey Please, Can't Ya See
  Barry White

You're My Baby
  Barry White

SIDE TWO
Hard to Believe That I Found You
  Barry White

Never, Never Gonna Give Ya Up
  Barry White

BARRY WHITE
Can't Get Enough
(1974)

Produced by: Barry White
20th CENTURY RECORDS, a subsidiary of 20th Century Fox Film Corporation

SIDE ONE

Mellow Mood (Part I)
Barry White/Tom Brock/Robert Taylor

You're the First, the Last, My Everything
Barry White/Tony Sepe/Sterling Radcliffe

I Can't Believe You Love Me
Barry White

SIDE TWO

Can't Get Enough of Your Love, Babe
Barry White

Oh Love, Well We Finally Made It
Barry White

I Love You More Than Anything
(in This World Girl)
Barry White

Mellow Mood (Part II)
Barry White/Tom Brock/Robert Taylor

BARRY WHITE
Just Another Way to Say, I Love You
(1975)

Produced by: Barry White
20th CENTURY RECORDS, a subsidiary of 20th Century Fox Film Corporation

SIDE ONE

Heavenly, That's What You Are to Me
  Barry White

I'll Do for You Anything You Want Me To
  Barry White

All Because of You
  Barry White/Frank Wilson/Michael Nunes

Love Serenade (Part I)
  Barry White

SIDE TWO

What Am I Gonna Do with You
  Barry White

Let Me Live My Life Lovin' You, Babe
  Barry White

Love Serenade (Part II)
  Barry White

BARRY WHITE
Barry White's Greatest Hits, Volume I
(1975)

Produced by: Barry White
20TH CENTURY RECORDS, a subsidiary of 20th Century Fox Film Corporation

SIDE ONE

What Am I Gonna Do with You
  Barry White

You're the First, the Last, My Everything
  Barry White/Tony Sepe/Sterling Radcliffe

Can't Get Enough of Your Love, Babe
  Barry White

Honey Please, Can't Ya See
  Barry White

Love Serenade
  Barry White

SIDE TWO

Never, Never Gonna Give Ya Up
  Barry White

I'm Gonna Love You Just a Little More,
Baby
  Barry White

I've Found Someone
  Barry White

I've Got So Much to Give
  Barry White

Standing in the Shadows of Love
  Holland/Dozier/Holland

BARRY WHITE
Let the Music Play
(1976)

Produced by: Barry White
20TH CENTURY RECORDS, a subsidiary of 20th Century Fox Film Corporation

SIDE ONE

I Don't Know Where Love Has Gone
Barry White

If You Know, Won't You Tell Me
Barry White

I'm So Blue and You Are Too
Barry White

SIDE TWO

Baby, We Better Try to Get It Together
Barry White

You See the Trouble with Me
Barry White/Ray Parker, Jr.

Let the Music Play
Barry White

BARRY WHITE
Is This Watcha Wont?
(1976)

Produced by: Barry White
20TH CENTURY RECORDS, a subsidiary of 20th Century Fox Film Corporation

SIDE ONE

Don't Make Me Wait Too Long
Barry White

Your Love (So Good I Can Taste It)
Barry White

SIDE TWO

I'm Qualified to Satisfy You
Barry White

I Wanna Lay Down with You Baby
Barry White

Now I'm Gonna Make Love to You
Barry White

BARRY WHITE
Barry White Sings For Someone You Love
(1977)

Produced by: Barry White
20th CENTURY RECORDS, a subsidiary of 20th Century Fox Film Corporation

SIDE ONE

Playing Your Game, Baby
Austin Johnson/Smead Hudman

It's Ecstasy When You Lay Down Next
to Me
Nelson Pigford/Ekundayo Paris

You're So Good You're Bad
Aaron Schroeder/Jerry Ragovoy

SIDE TWO

Never Thought I'd Fall in Love with You
Ronald E. Coleman

You Turned My Whole World Around
Frank Wilson/Danny Pearson

Oh What a Night for Dancing
Barry White/Vance Wilson

Of All the Guys in the World
Barry White/Danny Pearson

BARRY WHITE
The Man
(1978)

Produced by: Barry White
20th CENTURY RECORDS, a subsidiary of 20th Century Fox Film Corporation

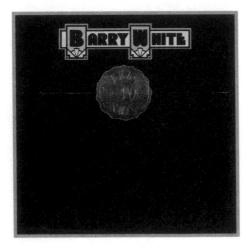

SIDE ONE

Look at Her
Frank Wilson/Raymond Cooksey/Tommy Payton

Your Sweetness Is My Weakness
Barry White

Sha La La Means I Love You
Barry White

SIDE TWO

September, When I First Met You
*Barry White/Frank Wilson/Paul Politi/
Ervin Brown*

It's Only Love Doing Its Thing
Jimmie Cameron/Vella Cameron

Just the Way You Are
Billy Joel

Early Years
Ronald Coleman

BARRY WHITE
I Love to Sing the Songs I Sing
(1979)

Produced by: Barry White
20th CENTURY RECORDS, a subsidiary of 20th Century Fox Film Corporation

SIDE ONE

I Love to Sing the Songs I Sing
Barry White/Paul Politi/Vance Wilson/Frank Wilson

Girl, What's Your Name
Barry White/Frank Wilson/Danny Pearson

Once Upon a Time (You Were a Friend of Mine)
Ronald Coleman

Oh Me, Oh My (I'm Such a Lucky Guy)
Barry White/Paul Politi/Raymond Cooksey/Frank Wilson

SIDE TWO

I Can't Leave You Alone
Barry White/Frank Wilson/Tony Sepe

Call Me, Baby
Ronald Coleman

How Did You Know It Was Me?
Ronald Coleman

BARRY WHITE
Barry White's Greatest Hits, Volume II
(1980)

Produced by: Barry White
20th CENTURY RECORDS, a subsidiary of 20th Century Fox Film Corporation

SIDE ONE

Love's Theme
Barry White

You See the Trouble with Me
Barry White/Ray Parker, Jr.

I'll Do for You Anything You Want Me To
Barry White

I'm Under the Influence of Love
Barry White/Paul Politi

Don't Make Me Wait Too Long
Barry White

SIDE TWO

Let the Music Play
Barry White

Baby, We Better Try to Get It Together
Barry White

It May Be Winter Outside
(But in My Heart It's Spring)
Barry White/Paul Politi

Bring Back My Yesterday
Barry White/Robert Relf

I'm Qualified to Satisfy You
Barry White

BARRY WHITE
The Message Is Love
(1979)

Executive Producer: Barry White
UNLIMITED GOLD RECORDS, INC.

SIDE ONE

It Ain't Love, Babe (Until You Give It Up)
Barry White/Paul Politi

Hung Up in Your Love
Barry White/Paul Politi

You're the One I Need
Barry White/Smead Hudman

Any Fool Could See (You Were Meant for Me)
Barry White/Paul Politi

SIDE TWO

Love Ain't Easy
Barry White/Paul Politi

I'm on Fire
Robert Jason

I Found Love
Barry White/Paul Politi

BARRY WHITE
The Best of Love
(1980)

Produced by: Barry White
UNLIMITED GOLD RECORDS, INC.

SIDE ONE

I Love to Sing the Songs I Sing
Barry White/Paul Politi/Vance Wilson/Frank Wilson

Let Me Live My Life Lovin' You, Babe
Barry White

It's Ecstasy When You Lay Down Next
to Me
Ekundayo Paris/Nelson Pigford

I'm Gonna Love You Just a Little More,
Baby
Barry White

Can't Get Enough of Your Love, Babe
Barry White

SIDE TWO

You're the First, the Last, My Everything
Barry White/Tony Sepe/Sterling Radcliffe

You See the Trouble with Me
Barry White/Ray Parker, Jr.

Playing Your Game, Baby
Smead Hudman/Austin Johnson

September, When I First Met You
Barry White/Paul Politi/Ervin Brown/Frank Wilson

Just the Way You Are
Billy Joel

BARRY WHITE
Barry White's Sheet Music
(1980)

Executive Producer: Barry White
UNLIMITED GOLD RECORDS, INC.

SIDE ONE

Sheet Music
Barry White/Paul Politi

Lady, Sweet Lady
Norman Sallitt

I Believe In Love
Barry White/Austin Johnson/Smead Hudman

SIDE TWO

Ghetto Letto
Barry White/Paul Politi/Vella Maria Cameron

Rum and Coke
*Morey Amsterdam/Jeri Sullavan/Paul Baron/
Al Stillman*

She's Everything to Me
Barry White/Bernard Butler

Love Makin' Music
Aaron Schroeder/Jerry Ragovoy

BARRY & GLODEAN
Barry & Glodean
(1981)

Produced by: Barry White
UNLIMITED GOLD RECORDS, INC.

SIDE ONE

Our Theme—Part I
Barry White

I Want You
Lowrell Simon/James Grigsby/Barry White

You're the Only One for Me
Barry White/Vella M. Cameron

This Love
Fleming Williams

The Better Love Is (the Worse It Is When
It's Over)
Adryan Russ

SIDE TWO

You
Barry White/Vella M. Cameron

We Can't Let Go of Love
Brent Maglia/Vito Giovanelli/Barry White

You Make My Life Easy Livin'
Vella M. Cameron/Jasper Cameron

Didn't We Make It Happen Baby
Barry White/Danny Pearson

Our Theme—Part II
Barry White

BARRY WHITE
Beware!
(1981)

Produced by: Barry White
UNLIMITED GOLD RECORDS, INC.

SIDE ONE

Beware
Jo Ann Belvin

Relax to the Max
Lowrell Simon/Barry White

Let Me In and Let's Begin with Love
Barry White/Vella Cameron

Your Love, Your Love
Lowrell Simon/Barry White

Tell Me Who Do You Love
Darnell White/Barry White

SIDE TWO

Rio de Janeiro
Marlon Jackson/Carol Jackson/Barry White

You're My High
Nathan East/Barry White

Oooo . . . Ahhh . . .
Fleming Williams/Barry White/Jakki Milligan

I Won't Settle for Less Than the Best (for You Baby)
Barry White/Vella M. Cameron

Louie, Louie
Richard Berry

BARRY WHITE
Change
(1982)

Executive Producer: Barry White
UNLIMITED GOLD RECORDS, INC.

SIDE ONE

Change
Barry White/Carl Taylor/John Lopez

Turnin' On, Tunin' In (to Your Love)
Vella M. Cameron

Let's Make Tonight (an Evening to
Remember)
Vella M. Cameron/Jasper Cameron

Don't Tell Me About Heartaches
Nat Kipner/John Vallins

SIDE TWO

Passion
Carl Taylor/Barry White/John Lopez

I've Got That Love Fever
Barry White/Jack Perry/Vella M. Cameron

I Like You, You Like Me
Barry White/Jack Perry

It's All About Love
Vella M. Cameron

BARRY WHITE
Dedicated
(1983)

Produced by: Barry White
UNLIMITED GOLD RECORDS, INC.

SIDE ONE

America
  Barry White

Free
  Barry White/Carl Taylor/Ricky Roberson

Don't Forget . . . Remember
  Barry White

Life
  Barry White/Jack Perry

SIDE TWO

Love Song
  Leslie Duncan

All in the Run of a Day
  Barry White/Robert Staunton

Don't Let 'Em Blow Your Mind
  Barry White/Jack Perry

Dreams
  Webster Lewis/Barry White

BARRY WHITE
The Right Night & Barry White
(1987)

Produced by: Barry White
A&M RECORDS, INC.

SIDE ONE
Sho' You Right
Barry White/Jack Perry

For Your Love
(I'll Do Most Anything)
Barry White/Bryan Loren

There's a Place (Where Love Never Ends)
Barry White/Frieda Brock/Doug Lambert

Love Is in Your Eyes
Barry White/Doug Williams/Jack Perry

Theme
Barry White/Doug Lambert

SIDE TWO
The Right Night
Barry White

I'm Ready for Love
Barry White/Edward Martinez/Doug Lambert

Theme (Sign of Love)
Barry White/Doug Lambert

Share
Barry White/Charles Fearing

Who's the Fool
Barry White/Jack Perry/Eugene Booker

BARRY WHITE
The Man Is Back!
(1989)

Produced by: Barry White
*Produced by: Barry White and Attala Zane Giles
A&M Records, Inc.

<table>
<tr><td>

SIDE ONE

Responsible
  Barry White/Julian Jackson/Jack Perry

Super Lover*
  Barry White/Jack Perry/William Jones

L.A. My Kinda Place
  Barry White

Follow That and See (Where It Leads Y'All)
  Barry White

When Will I See You Again
  Barry White/Terence Thomas

</td><td>

SIDE TWO

I Wanna Do It Good to Ya
  Barry White/Frank Rusty Hamilton III

It's Getting Harder All the Time
  Aaron Schroeder/David Grover

Don't Let Go
  Barry White/Terence Thomas/Eugene Booker

Love's Interlude/Good Night My Love
  Barry White/Grace Motola/John Marascalco

</td></tr>
</table>

BARRY WHITE
Put Me in Your Mix
(1991)

Produced by: Barry White
Coproduced by: Jack Perry
Associate Producer on "Put Me In Your Mix": Howard Johnson
A&M Records, Inc.

SIDE ONE	SIDE TWO
Let's Get Busy	**Put Me in Your Mix**
Barry White/Carl Taylor/Albert Lucero/ John Lopez	*Barry White/Howard Johnson*
Love Is Good with You	**Who You Giving Your Love To**
Barry White/Jack Perry/W.T. Jones	*Barry White*
For Real Chill	**Love Will Find Us**
Barry White/Jack Perry	*Barry White/Jack Perry*
Break It Down with You	**We're Gonna Have It All**
Barry White/Gordon Banks/Melvin Ragin	*Barry White/Aaron Schroeder/David Grover*
Volare	**Dark and Lovely (You Over There)**
Domenico Modugno/F. Migliacci/Mitchell Parsh	*Barry White*

BARRY WHITE
The Icon Is Love
(1994)

Produced and arranged by: Barry White and Jack Perry
A&M RECORDS, INC.

SIDE ONE

Practice What You Preach
Barry White/Gerald Levert/Edwin "Tony" Nicholas

There It Is
Barry White/Gerald Levert/Edwin "Tony" Nicholas

I Only Want to Be with You
Barry White/James Harris III/Terry Lewis

The Time Is Right
Barry White/Chuckii Booker

Baby's Home
Barry Eastmond/Gary Brown/Jolyon Skinner

SIDE TWO

Come On
Barry White/James Harris III/Terry Lewis

Love Is the Icon
Barry White/Jack Perry

Sexy Undercover
Barry White/Chuckii Booker

Don't You Want to Know?
Barry White/Michael Lovesmith

Whatever We Had, We Had
Barry White/Michael Lovesmith

BARRY WHITE
Just for You (box set)
(1992)

Songs Produced by: Barry White
Compilation Produced by: Barry White and Harry Weinger
MERCURY RECORDS

VOLUME 1

Prologue (Love's Beginning)

Barry White

Love's Theme

Barry White
Performed by Love Unlimited Orchestra
Single released November 1973
#10 R&B, #1 Pop

I'm Gonna Love You Just a Little More, Baby

Barry White
Single released February 1973
#1 R&B, #3 Pop

Never, Never Gonna Give Ya Up

Barry White
Single released September 1973
#2 R&B, #7 Pop

Can't Get Enough of Your Love, Babe

Barry White
Single released July 1974
#1 R&B, #1 Pop

You're the First, the Last, My Everything

Barry White/Tony Sepe/Sterling Radcliffe
Single released October 1974
#1 R&B, #2 Pop

What Am I Gonna Do with You

Barry White
Single released February 1975
#1 R&B, #8 Pop

Let the Music Play

Barry White
Single released December 1975
#4 R&B, #32 Pop

You See the Trouble with Me

Barry White/Ray Parker, Jr.
Single released February 1976
#14 R&B

Honey Please, Can't Ya See

Barry White
Single released January 1974
#6 R&B, #44 Pop

Don't Make Me Wait Too Long

Barry White
Single released October 1976
#20 R&B

It's Ecstasy When You Lay Down Next to Me

Nelson Pigford/Ekundayo Paris
Single released July 1977
#1 R&B, #4 Pop, #5 Disco

Your Sweetness Is My Weakness

Barry White
#2 R&B, #60 Pop, #16 Disco

L.A. My Kinda Place

Barry White

VOLUME 2

My Sweet Summer Suite

Barry White
Performed by Love Unlimited Orchestra
Single released August 1976
#28 R&B, #48 Pop

Change

Barry White/Carl Taylor/John Lopez
Single released July 1982
#12 R&B

Sho' You Right

Barry White/Jack Perry
Single released September 1987
#17 R&B

Sheet Music

Barry White/Paul Politi
Single released March 1980
#43 R&B

Love Makin' Music

Aaron Schroeder/Jerry Ragovoy
Single released June 1980
#25 R&B

Playing Your Game, Baby

Smead Hudman/Austin Johnson
Single released January 1978
#8 R&B

continued

It's Only Love Doing Its Thing
Vella Cameron/Jimmie Cameron

Love Serenade (Part I)
Barry White

Baby Blues
Barry White/Tony Sepe/Matty Brooks
Performed by Love Unlimited Orchestra

I've Got So Much to Give
Barry White
Single released June 1973
#5 R&B, #32 Pop

I've Found Someone
Barry White

Oh What a Night for Dancing
Barry White/Vance Wilson
Single released December 1977
#13 R&B, #24 Pop

VOLUME 3

Satin Soul
Barry White
Performed by Love Unlimited Orchestra
Single released January 1975
#23 R&B, #22 Pop

It Ain't Love, Babe (Until You Give It Up)
Barry White/Paul Politi
Single released June 1979
#58 R&B

I'll Do for You Anything You Want Me To
Barry White
Single released May 1975
#4 R&B, #40 Pop

Rio de Janeiro
Barry White/Marlon Jackson/Carol Jackson

All Around the World
Lisa Stansfield/Ian Devaney/Andy Morris
Performed by Barry White and Lisa Stansfield

Midnight and You
Gene Page/Billy Page
Performed by Love Unlimited Orchestra

Walkin' in the Rain with the One I Love
Barry White
Performed by Love Unlimited
Single released March 1972
#6 R&B, #14 Pop

Just the Way You Are
Billy Joel
Single released December 1978
#45 R&B

Beware
Jesse Belvin
Single released October 1981
#49 R&B

Who's the Fool
Barry White/Jack Perry/Eugene Booker

The Secret Garden (Sweet Seduction Suite)
Quincy Jones/Rod Temperton/Siedah Garrett/
El DeBarge
Peformed by Quincy Jones featuring Al B. Sure, James
Ingram, El DeBarge, and Barry White
Single released February 1990
#1 R&B, #31 Pop, #26 Adult Contemporary

All of Me
Barry White/Big Daddy Kane/Andre Booth
Performed by Big Daddy Kane featuring Barry White
Single released January 1991
#14 R&B

Dark and Lovely
Barry White
Performed by Barry White and Isaac Hayes
Single released January 1992
#29 R&B

Love's Interlude/Good Night My Love
Barry White/George Motola/John Marascalco

BARRY WHITE
All-Time Greatest Hits
(1994)

Produced by: Barry White
Compilation Produced by: Barry White and Harry Weinger
MERCURY RECORDS

Love's Theme
Barry White

I'm Gonna Love You Just a Little
More, Baby
Barry White

I've Got So Much to Give
Barry White

Never, Never Gonna Give Ya Up
Barry White

Honey Please, Can't Ya See
Barry White

Can't Get Enough of Your Love, Babe
Barry White

You're the First, the Last, My Everything
Barry White/Tony Sepe/Sterling Radcliffe

What Am I Gonna Do with You
Barry White

I'll Do for You Anything You Want Me To
Barry White

Let the Music Play
Barry White

You See the Trouble with Me
Barry White/Ray Parker, Jr.

Baby, We Better Try to Get It Together
Barry White

Don't Make Me Wait Too Long
Barry White

I'm Qualified to Satisfy You
Barry White

It's Ecstasy When You Lay Down Next
to Me
Ekundayo Paris/Nelson Pigford

Playing Your Game, Baby
Austin Johnson/Smead Hudman

Oh What a Night for Dancing
Barry White/Vance Wilson

Your Sweetness Is My Weakness
Barry White

Just the Way You Are
Billy Joel

Satin Soul
Barry White

BARRY WHITE
Staying Power
(1999)

Produced by: Barry White
PRIVATE MUSIC

SIDE ONE

Staying Power
Joey Paschal/Rory Holmes

The Longer We Make Love
Aaron Schroeder/Barry White/Marlon Saunders

Don't Play Games
Barry White/Jack Perry/Steve Guillory

I Get Off on You
Barry White/Jack Perry/Kashif

Which Way Is Up
Barry White/Jack Perry/Doug Rasheed

SIDE TWO

Get Up
Barry White/Jack Perry

Sometimes
Barry White

Low Rider
Harold Brown/Thomas Allen/Howard Scott/Charles Miller/Lee Levitin/LeRoy Jordan/Gerald Goldstein/Morris Dickerson

Thank You
Stewart Sylvester

Slow Your Roll
Barry White/Jack Perry/Joey Paschal

LOVE UNLIMITED ORCHESTRA
DISCOGRAPHY

LOVE UNLIMITED ORCHESTRA
Rhapsody in White
(1974)

Produced by: Barry White
20th CENTURY RECORDS, a subsidiary of 20th Century Fox Film Corporation

SIDE ONE

Barry's Theme
Barry White

Rhapsody in White
Barry White

Midnight and You
Gene Page/Billy Page

I Feel Love Coming On
Barry White/Paul Politi

SIDE TWO

Baby Blue
Barry White/Tony Sepe/Marty Brooks

Don't Take It Away from Me
Barry White

What a Groove
Barry White

Love's Theme
Barry White

LOVE UNLIMITED ORCHESTRA
Together Brothers (Original Motion Picture Soundtrack)
(1974)

Produced by: Barry White
20th CENTURY RECORDS, a subsidiary of 20th Century Fox Film Corporation

SIDE ONE

Somebody's Gonna Off the Man
Barry White

So Nice to Hear
Barry White

Alive and Well
Barry White

Find the Man Bros.
Barry White

You Gotta Case
Barry White

Killer's Lullaby
Barry White

Theme From *Together Brothers*
Barry White

Getaway
Barry White

People of Tomorrow Are the Children of
Today (Instrumental)
Barry White

SIDE TWO

Somebody's Gonna Off the Man
(Instrumental)
Barry White

The Rip
Barry White

Stick Up
Barry White

Dreamin'
Barry White

Killer's Back
Barry White

Do Drop In
Barry White

Killer Don't Do It
Barry White

Here Comes the Man
Barry White

Dream On
Barry White

Honey Please, Can't Ya See
Barry White

Can't Seem to Find Him
Barry White/Gene Page

People of Tomorrow Are the Children of
Today
Barry White

LOVE UNLIMITED ORCHESTRA
White Gold
(1974)

Produced by: Barry White
20th CENTURY RECORDS, a subsidiary of 20th Century Fox Film Corporation

SIDE ONE

Barry's Love (Part I)
Barry White

Satin Soul
Barry White

Always Thinking of You
Ray Parker, Jr.

Power of Love
Barry White/Tom Brock

Spanish Lei
Gene Page/Billy Page

SIDE TWO

You Make Me Feel Like This
(When You Touch Me)
Barry White

Only You Can Make Me Blue
Barry White

Dreaming
Barry White

Just Living It Up
Barry White

Just Like a Baby
Barry White/Gene Page

Barry's Love (Part II)
Barry White

LOVE UNLIMITED ORCHESTRA
Music Maestro Please
(1975)

Produced by: Barry White
20th CENTURY RECORDS, a subsidiary of 20th Century Fox Film Corporation

SIDE ONE

Bring It On Up
Barry White/Andrew Kastner/George Sopuch

Makin' Believe That It's You
Barry White/E. North Jr.

I Wanna Stay
Barry White

Give Up Your Love
Barry White/Delancy White

SIDE TWO

You're All I Want
Barry White

It's Only What I Feel
Barry White/Vance Wilson

Midnight Groove
Barry White/W. Seastrunk

Forever in Love
Barry White

LOVE UNLIMITED ORCHESTRA
My Sweet Summer Suite
(1976)

Produced by: Barry White
20th CENTURY RECORDS, a subsidiary of 20th Century Fox Film Corporation

SIDE ONE

My Sweet Summer Suite
Barry White

Strange Games and Things
Barry White

Blues Concerto
Barry White

You I Adore
Barry White/Tony Sepe

SIDE TWO

Brazilian Love Song
Barry White

Are You Sure
Glodean James/Linda James/Diane Taylor

You're Givin' Me Something
Barry White/Frank Wilson

I'm Fallin' in Love with You
Barry White

LOVE UNLIMITED ORCHESTRA
My Musical Bouquet
(1978)

Produced by: Barry White
20th CENTURY RECORDS, a subsidiary of 20th Century Fox Film Corporation

SIDE ONE

Don't You Know How Much I Love You
John Mayer

Stay Please and Make Love to Me
Barry White/Tony Sepe

Hey Look at Me, I'm in Love
Barry White/Delancy White

SIDE TWO

Love You, Ooh It's True Love
Barry White/Erwin Brown

Whisper Softly
Barry White/Vance Wilson

Enter Love's Interlude
Barry White/Vance Wilson

Can't You See
Barry White/Vance Wilson

LOVE UNLIMITED ORCHESTRA
Super Movie Themes, Just a Little Bit Different
(1979)

Arranged by: Barry White and Gene Page
20th CENTURY RECORDS, a subsidiary of 20th Century Fox Film Corporation

SIDE ONE

Theme from *Superman*
John Williams

Theme from *King Kong*
John Barry

Night Fever
Gibb/Gibb/Gibb

Grease
Barry Gibb

Intermission
Barry White

SIDE TWO

Theme from *Shaft*
Isaac Hayes

Theme from *A Summer Place*
Max Steiner

The Way We Were
Marvin Hamlish/Marilyn Bergman

As Time Goes By
Herman Hupfield

People of Tomorrow Are the Children
of Today
Barry White

LOVE UNLIMITED ORCHESTRA
Let 'Em Dance!
(1981)

Executive Producer: Barry White
UNLIMITED GOLD RECORDS, INC.

SIDE ONE

Bayou
Barry White

Jamaican Girl
Barry White

I Wanna Boogie and Woogie with You
Barry White

SIDE TWO

Vieni Qua Bella Mi
Barry White/Tony Sepe

Freeway Flyer
Barry White/Vance Wilson

I'm in the Mood
Barry White/Vance Wilson

Young America
*Barry White/Edwardo Rosado/Tony Sepe/
Donald Peake*

THE LOVE UNLIMITED ORCHESTRA PRESENTS
MR. WEBSTER LEWIS
Welcome Aboard
(1981)

Produced by: Barry White
UNLIMITED GOLD RECORDS, INC.

SIDE ONE

Welcome Aboard
Elwin Rutledge/Barry White/Jack Perry

Dreams
Webster Lewis/Barry White

Night Life in the City
Carl Taylor/Barry White

Lift Your Voice and Say (United We Can
Live in Peace Today)
Webster Lewis/Barry White

Welcome Aboard (Reprise)
Elwin Rutledge/Barry White/Jack Perry

SIDE TWO

Easin'
Nathan East/Barry White

Antigua Blue
Rudy Clarke/Barry White

Wind
Jimmy Cameron

Strange
Darnell White/Barry White

My Fantasies
Darnell White/Barry White

LOVE UNLIMITED ORCHESTRA
Rise
(1983)

Produced by: Barry White
UNLIMITED GOLD RECORDS, INC.

SIDE ONE

Take a Good Look (and What Do You See?)

Barry White/Carl Taylor/John Lopez

My Laboratory (Is Ready for You)

Barry White/Jack Perry/Vella Cameron

After Five

Barry White/Albert Carter

SIDE TWO

Do It to the Music . . . Please

Barry White/Jack Perry/Vella Cameron

In Brazil

Barry White/Jack Perry

Anna Lisa

Barry White/Al McKay

Goodbye Concerto

Barry White/Albert Testa/Tony DeVita

LOVE UNLIMITED ORCHESTRA
The Best of Love Unlimited Orchestra
(1995)

Produced and Conducted by: Barry White
Compilation produced by: Barry White and Harry Weinger
MERCURY RECORDS

My Sweet Summer Suite
Barry White

Don't You Know How Much I Love You
John Mayer

Brazilian Love Song
Barry White

Rhapsody in White
Barry White

Love's Theme
Barry White

Satin Soul
Barry White

Theme from *Together Brothers*
Barry White

Theme from *King Kong*
John Barry

Bring It on Up
Barry White/Andrew Kastner/George Sopuch

Blues Concerto
Barry White

Let the Music Play (Instrumental)
Barry White

Forever in Love
Barry White

Midnight and You
Gene Page/Billy Page

Can't You See
Barry White/Vance Wilson

Baby Blues
Barry White/Tony Sepe

LOVE UNLIMITED
DISCOGRAPHY

ALBUM	RELEASE DATE
UNI	
1. From a Girl's Point of View We Give to You . . .	1972
20th Century Records	
2. Under the Influence Of . . .	1973
3. In Heat	1974
Unlimited Gold Records, Inc.	
4. He's All I've Got	1977
5. Love Is Back	1979

LOVE UNLIMITED
From a Girl's Point of View We Give to You . . .
(1972)

Produced by: Barry White
UNI RECORDS, INC.

SIDE ONE

I Should Have Known
Barry White/Robert Relf

Another Chance
Barry White/Tom Brocker

Are You Sure
Linda James/Diane Taylor/Glodean James

Fragile—Handle with Care
Barry White

SIDE TWO

I'll Be Yours Forever More
Barry White

If This World Were Mine
Marvin Gaye

Together
Kevin Gamble/Leon Huff

Walkin' in the Rain with the One I Love
Barry White

LOVE UNLIMITED
Under the Influence Of . . .
(1973)

Produced by: Barry White
20th CENTURY RECORDS, a subsidiary of 20th Century Fox Film Corporation

SIDE ONE

Love's Theme (Instrumental)
Barry White

Under the Influence of Love
Barry White/Paul Politi

Lovin' You, That's All I'm After
Barry White

Oh Love, Well We Finally Made It
Barry White

SIDE TWO

Say It Again
Barry White

Someone Really Cares for You
Barry White

It May Be Winter Outside (But in My Heart It's Spring)
Barry White/Paul Politi

Yes, We Finally Made It
Barry White

LOVE UNLIMITED
In Heat
(1974)

Produced by: Barry White
20th CENTURY RECORDS, a subsidiary of 20th Century Fox Film Corporation

SIDE ONE

Move Me No Mountain
  Aaron Schroeder/Jerry Ragavoy

Share a Little Love in Your Heart
  Barry White

Oh, I Should Say, It's Such a Beautiful Day
  Barry White

SIDE TWO

I Needed Love You Were There
  Barry White

I Belong to You
  Barry White

I Love You So, I'm Never Gonna Let You Go
  Barry White

Love's Theme
  Barry White/Aaron Schroeder

LOVE UNLIMITED
He's All I've Got
(1977)

Produced by: Barry White
UNLIMITED GOLD RECORDS, INC.

SIDE ONE

I Did It for Love
  Linda Lurie/Terri Etlinger

Never, Never Say Goodbye
  Barry White

Whisper You Love Me
  Barry White

He's Mine (No, You Can't Have Him)
  Barry White

SIDE TWO

I Can't Let Him Down
  Barry White

I Guess I'm Just Another Girl in Love
  Barry White

He's All I've Got
  Barry White

LOVE UNLIMITED
Love Is Back
(1979)

Executive Producer: Barry White
UNLIMITED GOLD RECORDS, INC.

SIDE ONE

I'm So Glad That I'm a Woman
Barry White/Frank Wilson/Paul Politi

High Steppin' Hip Dressin' Fella (You Got It Together)
Barry White/Frank Wilson/Paul Politi

When I'm in Your Arms, Everything's Okay
Barry White/Frank Wilson/Paul Politi

SIDE TWO

If You Want Me, Say It
Barry White/Frank Wilson/Paul Politi

I'm Givin' You a Love (Every Man Is Searchin' For)
Barry White/Frank Wilson/Paul Politi

Gotta Be Where You Are
Barry White

I'm His Woman
Barry White/Barbara Borde/Paul Politi

PHOTO CAPTIONS
AND CREDITS

Page ii: Photo courtesy of Barry White.

Page v: Here I am with my beautiful mother, Sadie, who was visiting me in the studio for an afternoon in the '80s while I was recording one my albums. *Photo courtesy of Barry White.*

Page 3: This is me at the age of five on my Hopalong Cassidy bicycle, which was a present from my mom and dad. This is also the same year I started playing the piano. *Photo courtesy of Barry White.*

Page 7: My dad, Melvin Arthur White, was quite the dapper fellow. *Photo courtesy of Barry White.*

Page 8: I'm three years old here. My father took this photo for his wallet and family collection. *Photo courtesy of Barry White.*

Page 11: This is me at the age of nine. I'm the taller one; my brother, Darryl, was eight. Behind us is my father's 1949 Mercury. *Photo courtesy of Barry White.*

Page 29: This is my publicity photo from 1973, which we used when I released my first album, *I've Got So Much to Give. Photo courtesy of Barry White.*

Page 40: This is one of my favorite photos. It was taken in 1974, while I was on the road. *Photo courtesy of Barry White.*

Page 65: Here I am performing at a 1981 benefit in my "own back yard"—Inglewood, California. *Photo courtesy of Barry White.*

Page 85: Linda, Glodean, me, and Diana on the set of *Soul Train* in 1972. *Photo courtesy of Barry White.*

Page 93: Glodean, with the long fingernails she was known for, and me at an awards dinner sometime in the '70s. *Photo courtesy of Barry White.*

Page 95: Me, Glodean, and Stevie Wonder in 1975 at the NAACP Awards party. *Photo courtesy of Barry White.*

Page 105: Linda, Glodean, and Diana. *Photo courtesy of Barry White.*

Page 106: From the cover of my album *I've Got So Much to Give,* 1973. *Photo courtesy of Barry White.*

Page 113: This is me performing at the Royal Albert Hall in London, 1974. I love my British fans! *Photo courtesy of Barry White.*

Page 126: This was taken at the waterfalls of my Sherman Oaks Estate, which I purchased from the great Larry Nunes. This was part of a photo shoot I was doing for the release of *Barry White Sings for Someone You Love.*

Page 136: Truly the Greatest—Muhammad Ali. We're backstage after a concert at the Greek Theater in L.A. *Photo by Howard L. Bingham.*

Page 138: Left to right: Quincy Jones, Marvin Hagler, and me at the Universal Amphitheater in Los Angeles after a 1990 concert of mine. *Photo by Lester Cohen.*

Page 146: My beautiful children. Top row, left to right: Kevin, Darryl, Barry, Jr.; bottom row: Denise, Bridget, Shaherah, Lanese, Nina.

Page 164: Photo courtesy of Barry White.

Page 167: One of the proudest days of my life came when I received this honorary doctorate from Paul Quinn College. *Photo courtesy of Barry White.*

Page 172: Me and Glodean, 1981. *Photo courtesy of Barry White.*

Page 174: Somewhere in Europe during *The Icon Is Love* Tour, 1995. *Photo courtesy of Barry White.*

Page 180: Here I am standing before the Sphinx and the Great Pyramids of Egypt, 1993. *Photo courtesy of Barry White.*

Page 189: My close friend and musical cohort Jack Perry with Puff Daddy and me in 1998 during a break in the recording of my new album *Staying Power. Photo courtesy of Jack Perry.*

Page 193: The great Lisa Stansfield in 1990 and me after recording *All Around the World. Photo courtesy of Barry White.*

Page 196: Miss Katherine Denton and me. *Photo by Greg Gorman.*

PERMISSIONS

Practice What You Preach
Words and Music by Barry White, Gerald Levert, and Edwin "Tony" Nicholas
© 1994 Seven Songs
Administered by A. Schroeder International Ltd., Divided Music Inc. (Admin. By Zomba Songs, Inc.), Warner-Tamerlane Publishing Corp. and Ramal Music Co. (Admin. By Warner-Tamerlane Publishing Corp.)
Used by Permission, International Copyright Secured

Staying Power
Words and Music by Joey Paschal and Rory Holmes
© 1997 Seven Songs
Administered by A. Schroeder International Ltd.
Used by Permission, International Copyright Secured

It's Ecstasy When You Lay Down Next to Me
Words and Music by Ekundayo Paris and Nelson Pigford
© 1977 Ba-Dake Music, Inc.
Administered by A. Schroeder International Ltd.
Used by Permission, International Copyright Secured

I'm So Glad That I'm a Woman
Words and Music by Barry White, Frank Wilson and Paul Politi
© 1979 Seven Songs and Ba-Dake Music, Inc.
Administered by A. Schroeder International Ltd.
Used by Permission, International Copyright Secured

Love Ain't Easy
Words and Music by Barry White and Paul Politi
© 1979 Seven Songs and Ba-Dake Music, Inc.
Administered by A. Schroeder International Ltd.
Used by Permission, International Copyright Secured

I've Got So Much to Give
Words and Music by Barry White
© 1973 Savette Music Co. (BMI) and Unichappell Music, Inc. (BMI)
All Rights Administered by Unichappell Music, Inc. (BMI)
All Rights Reserved. Used by Permission.

Never, Never Gonna Give Ya Up
Words and Music by Barry White
© 1973 Savette Music Co. (BMI) and Unichappell Music, Inc. (BMI)
All Rights Administered by Unichappell Music, Inc. (BMI)
All Rights Reserved. Used by Permission.

I've Found Someone
Words and Music by Barry White
© 1973 Savette Music Co. (BMI), Six Continents Music, January Music Corp. (BMI) and Unichappell Music, Inc. (BMI)
All Rights Reserved. Used by Permission.

Can't Get Enough of Your Love, Babe
Words and Music by Barry White
© 1974 Unichappell Music Inc. (BMI) and Savette Music Co. (BMI)
All Rights on behalf of Savette Music Co. (BMI) Administered by Unichappell Music, Inc. (BMI)
All Rights Reserved. Used by Permission.

I'm Gonna Love You Just a Little More, Baby
Words and Music by Barry White
© 1973 Unichappell Music Inc. (BMI) and Savette Music Co. (BMI)
All Rights on behalf of Savette Music Co. (BMI) Administered by Unichappell Music, Inc. (BMI)
All Rights Reserved. Used by Permission.